Passage Rites

Adversity's Challenge

Michael W. Crabtree

iUniverse, Inc.

New York Bloomington

Cover photograph courtesy of North Carolina State University Athletic Department. Used with permission.

iUniverse books may be ordered through booksellers or by contacting:

iUniverse
1663 Liberty Drive
Bloomington, IN 47403
www.iuniverse.com
1-800-Authors (1-800-288-4677)

Because of the dynamic nature of the Internet, any Web addresses or links contained in this book may have changed since publication and may no longer be valid. The views expressed in this work are solely those of the author and do not necessarily reflect the views of the publisher, and the publisher hereby disclaims any responsibility for them.

ISBN: 978-1-4502-5119-8 (sc)
ISBN: 978-1-4502-5121-1 (hc)
ISBN: 978-1-4502-5120-4 (ebook)

Printed in the United States of America

iUniverse rev. date: 10/13/2010

Dedicated to the memory of two special human beings: Bobby Wayne Crabtree and Alberta Anne "Sissy" Snyder Crabtree—my parents. Thank you for the understanding and patience. May your examples be promoted in cultures that all should mutually desire.

Contents

Introduction

My parents' fiftieth wedding anniversary reception was held on January 2, 2004, in a large hall that had been built years ago next to Church of the Ascension, in Virginia Beach, Virginia. We had had my parents' twenty-fifth anniversary reception in the church itself. Present now were many of the persons I had grown up with, and many adults who had watched me grow through my teenage years, until I started college at North Carolina State University. I felt self-conscious the entire evening, as my life had not gone as I had planned or hoped. In a way, I felt as though I had failed these persons.

I had driven from my home outside of Houston, Texas, to Virginia Beach to attend the reception, bringing my wife and four children. The youngest was sixteen, next oldest the seventeen-year-old twins, and my eldest, nineteen. When asked during the reception what I had been doing, I told of my last assignment in the oil exploration industry, working in Cape Town, South Africa. My next assignment, to begin in less than two weeks, was to be in Indonesia. I also told of my ongoing litigation involving a patent entitlement for an invention that I had first developed in Scotland before being transferred to Brazil five years previously.

Somehow, what I had accomplished was not enough, to me. My father approached me. He had noticed my discomfort at the reception. He told me not to have any regrets that my life had not turned out as I had planned. A brother and sister had become engineers, as I had planned to do, but I did not finish college. I had instead made a good living in the oil industry. However, it was a cyclical industry, and I had been through a bankruptcy after being laid off many years back. Between that and a divorce, I had to start over financially twice as an adult. My adult life had been a struggle, unlike that of my siblings. It was not supposed to be a struggle, in my plans. I had followed society's "recipe for success" as a young man.

I had become much more like my father in the period since the twenty-fifth anniversary reception. I now tended to speak little, and only when I felt a need to say something. I had become emotionally reserved, not really knowing how to express the side of me that had, years earlier, been so much more dominant.

Thinking back, the majority of the changes occurred in a relatively rapid period, from autumn 1976 through the first weeks of 1979. My life had gone terribly wrong, and I had little choice but to start over. Through the years, I had told my children and wife bits and pieces of the whole story. Now, in admitting to myself that my father's statement about regret was correct, I decided to publish the story of what occurred in that period.

I handwrote the original manuscript in 1980 and kept it in a footlocker in my closet. A few of the names have been changed in this text, but most have not. The story is true, of my passage to adulthood.

Michael W. Crabtree
Katy, Texas
February 2010

Changes: Who Are You?

The summer heat was intense, especially when in full football gear for summer practices. It was late August. NC State University's 1976 football season was to begin in less than two weeks. Coach Lou Holtz left the football program after the 1975 season, when the team finished the year ranked tenth in the country. We had played in the Peach Bowl, in Atlanta, on New Year's Eve of 1976. As a freshman, I was thrilled and excited by the whole thing, playing in front of more than seventy thousand people. I had spent years looking forward to such opportunities.

Bo Rein had taken over as head coach. He had different methods of coaching than Lou Holtz and was trying to make changes that more reflected his coaching philosophy. There had been some position changes, but nothing major. During the spring practices in 1976, I had earned a starting offensive position for the coming season.

The summer had gone much as expected. We had progressed from mere conditioning and play practicing to full-speed contact between the starting offensive and defensive players. Today was the last full contact before the first game. We broke from the huddle, and I trotted to my position as flanker. My friend and former roommate, Tom Ebner, lined up across from me as the defensive strong safety. Now sophomores, he and I had become fast friends from the start. The play to be run was a curling pass pattern, to me. Having stopped at my location in the offensive formation, I glanced at Tom before getting down into my set stance.

Tom was from Houston: a square-jawed, blonde-haired, blue-eyed Texan, six feet two inches tall, and two hundred-ten pounds. He was fast and physical. He outweighed me by thirty pounds, but I was quicker. In order to get open, I thought, I would need to try making Tom think I would go deep. I glanced at the quarterback, then back at Tom. He had taken two steps farther away from the line of scrimmage. This could be tough.

On the previous play, I faked a pattern to the inside and tried to break past Tom. He was caught by my fake and would have been beaten on the play had he not slammed a forearm into my chest as I tried to run past him. Now, giving himself more distance from me, it would be difficult for me to make Tom respect a deep pattern fake. The curl pattern would not give me sufficient room to do that.

The play began. I reached the practiced distance from the line of scrimmage, as a known number of steps. As I was about to turn, I could tell Tom had not given any ground. This would be close. I pivoted, absorbing momentum with my right leg to come to an almost halted position, knees slightly bent and legs apart, ready to locate the ball's position.

The ball had been thrown high. I did not think, only reacted. One of my athletic gifts had always been unusual leaping ability. I went up very high for the pass, stretching my arms as high as I could to gather in the ball. I felt the leather against my fingertips, looking at the ball coming into my hands. That is what we were taught: watch the ball all of the way into your hands.

I felt the sudden contact at the small of my back. Tom was driving his shoulder pad into me, to force me to drop the pass. Next was an abnormal movement. My torso and arms, above the impact point, momentarily remained where they were. My hips and legs, beneath the contact point, remained where they were. It was as if I was being folded backward at that one point in my spine. Tom drove forward as he was running. I felt something snap in my back.

I was still watching the ball as it was going through my hands. Tom's impact had forced my arms to splay apart, and the ball passed between my hands. My upper body pitched forward, and I looked first at the horizon level and then at the grass. My arms fell into position in front of my chest, slightly flexed to absorb the impending contact with the ground. Tom's momentum caused his body to move over mine as we both fell forward. He landed on top of me and rolled off. The impact caused me to exhale involuntarily. It took a moment to regain my breath.

Tom was quickly on his feet. "You all right, Crab?" Tom asked, using the nickname he had given me shortly after we met. He came over and reached down to help me up.

"I don't know," I replied, finding it difficult to breathe. I raised myself from the ground, kneeling on one knee. "Trainer!" I hollered. I continued kneeling as he approached. My breathing was returning to normal, and I did not feel any pain. Maybe I was okay. "I felt something give," I told him when he reached me. I stood up, placing my hands on my flexed knees, bent over.

"Is it hurting?" he asked.

"No."

"Where did you feel it?"

I reached my right hand back, running fingers near the base of my spine. "Here."

The trainer ran his hand lightly along my spine, feeling either side, perhaps for abnormal protrusions. He stopped after a few moments. "I don't feel anything. Try walking a bit, to see if you can feel anything different. We'll take a look at you after practice."

"We" didn't take a look at me after practice, at least not any physical examination. There was a little bit of soreness in the muscles just to the right of my spine. Cold compresses were applied for a while. I showered as usual and got dressed. During the remainder of summer practices, I applied hot and cold compresses. The aching in the muscles on one side did not subside.

I played the first game and was in pain afterward. My parents and an aunt and uncle had come to watch the game. I met them outside the locker room after the game. We had intended to go to dinner. Instead, I asked that they go themselves. I returned to my dorm room in pain.

Three days later, all I could feel in my right leg was pain. I had no muscular control of it. The collision with Tom Ebner had broken a bone near the base of my spine, and the nerves to my right leg were being compressed. I missed one game, in traction in the infirmary, and then played in the season's remaining games.

It is not something I regret, as the memories will remain with me until my last breath. I would always be thankful to NC State for the opportunity. The guys I played with were great guys. Some went on to play professional football. One, Bill Cowher, has gone on to coach the Pittsburgh Steelers to become Super Bowl Champions. We must sometimes make personal decisions that lead to uncharted territory. Having been told that another collision could permanently paralyze me, I finally decided to give up playing football. That meant giving up my athletic scholarship as well.

Always academically oriented, I was recruited by more than a dozen engineering colleges, Princeton, and the US Naval Academy. Instead, I chose North Carolina State University, which at the time was ranked fifth-best engineering college in the nation. It was where my father attended college. And it had one of the best football programs in the country, under Lou Holtz. Now I had consciously chosen to give that up, not knowing what the future might bring. I had no money to pay for college.

Looking back, more than thirty years later, there are no regrets. My father told me to not have any regrets, as what has evolved after those decisions is who I now am. He was correct. Regrets are for those who have surrendered or given up striving, who have chosen to cower in the "face of adversity," as Coach Holtz would say with his lisp. We are the decisions that we make: right or wrong, good or bad. The results may often require us to reassess priorities or directions. Ultimately, our individual lives unfold as stories we tell ourselves and earn among those with whom we live. And, they are the struggles that we face, whether or not our attempts to overcome them are successful.

In January 1978, I left my hometown of Virginia Beach, Virginia, with a backpack, one hundred dollars, a notebook of poems, and a guitar case. Tom Ebner, who had transferred to the University of Houston, had told me there was work in the oilfield, in Houston.

Hitchhiking to Houston took six memorable days. It was cold.

On my first day, in the countryside near Suffolk, Virginia, a minister gave me a ride. It lasted perhaps an hour. He asked the reason for my journey. I explained briefly that everything had gone terribly wrong. Who I had been, in the social contexts in which that person existed, no longer existed. I had to find out who I was outside of the contexts of the past.

The minister told me that sometimes persons had to give up the past in seeking their cores. The past could stand as a stage of illusory values and self-worth. There was no shame in taking the chance, he said, to find out who you are. When he came to the junction where he needed to leave the main road, he prayed for me and asked that God go with me. I thanked him for his concern, his kind words, and got out of the car. The wind blew, chilly and impersonal, as his car pulled away down the two-lane road.

The second day was spent seeing some friends in eastern North Carolina. The third day, I stopped in Burlington, North Carolina. What happened there convinced me to go on to Houston. That night, I slept in woods beside the interstate highway, near King Mountain, North Carolina.

It was cold and raining when I awoke. A portion of my sleeping bag was damp, having been protruding from beneath the plastic shower curtain I used as a ground cloth and top cover. Deeply chilled, I quickly dressed and headed down the hill to the service road running parallel to the interstate. Perhaps owing to the inclement weather, I was picked up by the first motorist coming by. He drove me to a truck stop, where hot coffee and a large breakfast warmed me.

I pulled some paper from my notebook and made an "Atlanta" sign. It helped immensely. Ten minutes' cold, damp, and hopefulness from the truck stop, a car pulled up to me. The driver was a member of a traveling rock band. He said he had played in Charlotte the previous night and was going to Birmingham, Alabama.

As we approached Birmingham, the roads were covered with snow. The weather forecast was overnight snow. I had run into the city's worst snowstorm in fifteen years. Even Interstate 20 was being closed due to the weather.

He wished me luck and dropped me off after exiting the interstate. The time was 5:30 PM. Darkness was beginning to settle upon the city. I glanced around, seeking some form of shelter and a place to eat. Although I could not distinctly see it from a distance due to shadows, the interstate overpass seemed to have a flat area at the top of the incline, where the main beams rested upon the concrete. One hundred yards away was a waffle shop.

I walked up the incline beneath the overpass. There was a ledge about six feet wide. I removed my backpack, hiding it and the guitar between two of the beams, well back into the shadows.

My sleeping bag was damp from the night before in King Mountain. My clothes were damp. I was shivering when I entered the waffle shop. How warm it was, dry. It felt so good. The few groups of people within looked at me as I entered. They grew momentarily quiet, watching, and then resumed their discussions. I took off my cap, sort of smoothing out the curly hair that had been flattened under the cap all day. I walked silently to a back booth in a corner. A large woman with reddish hair, fair complexion, and some freckles asked to take my order. I requested coffee and some time to read the menu. More than anything, I wanted warmth.

My hands were red from the cold, and I could only assume that my face was. I had dressed in layers and began removing my coat and sweater. Beneath them I wore coveralls, a long sleeve pullover shirt, and blue jeans. All were damp but could not be removed.

The waitress brought my coffee. "Where you from?" she asked. She was pretty, and her face displayed kindness.

"I left Virginia four days ago. I'm trying to make it to Houston, to find work."

"You sure picked the wrong time to arrive here," she began, pouring coffee into my cup. "The state troopers are going to close

I-20, and it's supposed to snow for the next two days. You might get lucky and catch something tonight, if you hurry."

I ordered eggs and bacon with toast and, as she walked away, pondered what to do. I was tired and really wanted to get some sleep before again embarking. I didn't want to sleep in the cold but did not have much money.

Short order cooks can do wonders with simple eggs, I thought as I devoured them, supposing that hunger had much to do with how good these eggs seemed to taste. I paid and quickly left, thanking the waitress. She wished me good luck.

Walking back to the overpass, I noticed a hotel farther along the road, on the other side of the overpass. I went up and got my backpack and guitar, heading for the hotel. Knowing that my clothing was damp, I wanted to sleep warm and dry that night. The hotel cost thirty dollars, not leaving me much for the remainder of the trip. I could make it, though, if I watched what I spent. My clothes and sleeping bag could dry overnight. If I got stuck another day here, I could sleep under the overpass the second night.

I put my backpack and guitar in the room and stripped off the outer garments, including the coveralls, putting them by a radiator on a side wall of the small, simple room. A bar shared the entrance by the hotel front desk. I decided I could treat myself to one beer.

Country music played in the background from an old jukebox. There were short candles on each table, in red glass goblets. The tables were square, wooden, and just large enough for four persons. There was a mirror behind the bar, and neon beer signs on the walls. I sat on a stool at the wooden bar, two seats over from a black-haired man who appeared to be about forty. I nodded in his direction as I sat down, acknowledging him as a gesture of respectful greeting, and ordered a draft beer.

"Can you believe this snow?" I asked him. "What a time to arrive in Birmingham."

"Yeah, I know," he replied. "I was supposed to be here for business tomorrow." He took a long sip from his mug. "But it looks like all of the roads and businesses will be closed."

"What do you do?" I asked.

"I'm in sales. I work Alabama, Mississippi, and Louisiana, based out of New Orleans."

The barmaid placed my beer on the counter. "That'll be a dollar fifty, for Happy Hour."

"Thanks," I told her. I gave her two dollars and told her to keep the change. The beer's dark taste was sharp and pleasant.

"Well," the salesman said. "If I don't make it out of here soon, I won't be going anywhere."

"Are you going to New Orleans?"

"Yeah," he replied, signaling to the barmaid for his bill.

"Could I catch a ride with you?" I earnestly asked. "I'm trying to make it to New Orleans, where I have a friend at Tulane University."

"I can't wait around," he stated.

"Give me ten minutes, please, mister," I pleaded. "All I have to do is grab my backpack."

"Okay," he replied. "I'll wait that long."

"Thanks!" I said.

I signaled the barmaid and told her I would be right back. I left the bar and returned to my room, put back on my outer clothing and coat, and grabbed my backpack and guitar. I went to the front desk and explained that I was not going to need the room, because I was leaving for New Orleans almost immediately. The front desk clerk, a young woman, didn't want to give me back my money. I told her I didn't have much money, and that I had not showered or even ruffled the bed covers. She finally conceded and gave me back the thirty dollars.

I walked back into the bar. The stranger was not there. "Excuse me, ma'am," I asked the barmaid. "Did the man who was here say he would be back?"

"No. He didn't say anything. He just paid and left."

I walked out of the bar and hotel to the parking lot. One space had been recently vacated, as the asphalt was not covered with snow, and fresh tire tracks were visible leading away from the space. *Crap*, I thought. The stranger was gone.

I walked dejectedly back into the bar, set down my backpack and guitar beside the barstool, and removed my coat. It appeared that it would be the hotel tonight after all. The bar was warm, cozy. I would finish my beer, and then go to the room and get some sleep. *What a day*, I reflected. It had begun in the rain on a North Carolina hillside and was ending in a snowbound Birmingham. Sipping the beer lasted about twenty minutes. There was nowhere else to go, so why hurry?

I again thanked the barmaid, gathered my coat, guitar and pack, and went back to the hotel front desk. "Ma'am," I told the clerk, "I'm afraid my ride to New Orleans fell through. I'm going to need that room."

"Well," she said, "I'm sorry to tell you this, but that room has been taken. We don't have any vacancies left."

"Oh, damn!" I exclaimed. I sighed in exasperation. "Well, thank you anyway."

Donning my coat and then the backpack, I exited the hotel and began trudging through the snow toward the overpass. The snow was by now more than four inches deep, crunching beneath my boots with each step. It glistened from the fluorescent street lights, and more snow fell past the lights from the dark grayish skies. Snow seemed to dampen sound, absorb it, even as it made a soft sound as it fell upon objects. The only other sounds were a few vehicles on the interstate, above me. The other streets were empty of traffic.

Climbing back up to the ledge beneath the overpass, I unrolled the sleeping bag. It would be better to sleep without clothing than to sleep in damp clothing. I undressed completely, placing the coat on top of the sleeping bag and the clothing within it, at the foot, then got into the bag. I was shivering. I looked at my watch, which had phosphorescent places on the minute and hour hands. It was only 8:30.

The last time I looked at the watch before sleeping it was ten o'clock, and I had been shivering the entire time, unable to sleep. When I next looked at the watch, my teeth were chattering, and I was shivering uncontrollably. It was just after 2:00 AM. My body told me that it was tired and needed to sleep, but my mind knew this could be dangerous. I could not allow myself to go back to sleep, not here.

Shaking violently, I put back on my clothes, stowing the pack, sleeping bag, and guitar back between the beams. My feet were freezing, my toes numb. The boots had become hard from the cold. Walking down the incline was difficult, even though there was no snow on it due to the overpass. My feet ached. My shivering made maintaining my balance difficult, as my legs felt like they were going to buckle.

The sign at the waffle shop was lit, and there were a few cars in the parking lot. I headed for it. Opening the door, I counted five customers, a waitress and the cook. Two customers were leaned over in booths, their eyes closed.

"Mind if I warm up a bit, ma'am?" I asked the waitress, a black woman perhaps in her late twenties. She was petite, but not really attractive. This was a job for her.

"No," she replied. "These other folks are stranded, too. Have a seat."

"Thank you, ma'am," I said. "Coffee, please." I went back to the same booth where I had earlier eaten. It seemed safe in that corner, facing everyone else in the place, my back to the farthest wall from the door. My fingers were numb, and unzipping the coat was difficult. I blew into my cupped hands several times before I was able to get sufficient grip on the heavy zipper to undo it. I placed the coat and sweater beside me on the seat.

The waitress brought the coffee cup and filled it. I placed my hands around it to warm them. It took a couple of minutes of warming in this way for me to be able to bend my finger around the handle and hold the cup with one hand. She continued to fill my cup for several hours as I warmed in the waffle shop.

During the night, I had heard vehicles occasionally passing on the road above me. Now that I was warmed, I decided to try catching a ride out of Birmingham. Leaving a generous tip, I left the restaurant and walked up the nearest entrance ramp to the interstate. There were large truck tire marks in the snow, although the snow completely covered the highway. In the waffle shop, I'd made another sign, this one reading "New Orleans." A tractor trailer began to come around the bend, about a half-mile away. It was moving fairly slowly, in the lane farthest from me. As it neared, I held up my sign. It did not slow.

I began walking along the highway, thinking that was the best way to keep warm. Ten minutes of walking passed. Then twenty minutes. A pickup truck was coming around that bend. It was in the lane nearest me. *Please stop*, I thought. I held up my sign, facing the truck's direction. Two hundred yards from me, the truck began to slow. Its back wheels stopped and the truck skidded, and the driver would allow the wheels to again roll. He repeated this sequence a number of times, finally coming to a full stop fifty yards past me. I ran to catch up to the truck.

I reached the truck. The driver was a middle-aged man with a graying mustache and beard. Beside him in the passenger seat was a teenage male.

"Can you give me a lift?" I asked.

"If you don't mind riding in the back," he answered. "You going to New Orleans?"

"I'm trying to. I didn't know if I would make it out of here today."

"We're only going as far as Meridian, but you can catch the interstate from there into New Orleans," he stated.

"I really appreciate this, sir," I said. "Honestly."

"Go ahead and hop in."

The truck bed was filled with snow. That didn't matter; this was my way out. I placed the guitar and backpack near the back of the bed and climbed in. I leaned back against a tire at the front of the bed, next to the back of the cab, using the cab as a wind block. The truck's tire spun a bit, but the man managed to get traction, and the truck slowly moved forward.

About fifty miles west of Birmingham, the snow had stopped. Farther west, the morning sky was clear. The snow looked pretty on the Alabama hillsides. It sparkled in the daylight. We exited Interstate 20 at Meridian, Mississippi. The temperature was in the upper forties. The driver told me to walk to the other side of the service roads for Interstate 59, which would go all the way into New Orleans. I repeatedly thanked the driver and watched the two head toward their destination.

Luck remained with me that morning as I soon had a ride headed all the way to New Orleans. The driver was a man from New Orleans, with a thick Cajun accent and curly dark hair. I told him about my journey to this point, and that I was going to Houston to find work. He was very friendly and open. Tom Ebner's girlfriend had been attending college at Tulane. Tom told me to contact her when I got to the campus, and she could arrange a stay with some friends or at a cheap guest dorm. The driver said his son was attending Tulane, and that he would give me a ride to the campus.

We talked the entire trip into New Orleans. This man had a great sense of humor and had some stories. It was a very enjoyable ride.

As we headed south toward New Orleans, the temperature got warmer. Arriving in New Orleans, the temperature was seventy-five degrees. The kind man dropped me off at the Tulane campus. He told me where the Registration building was, which was most likely where I could get contact information for Tom's girlfriend. I thanked him for the ride and for the conversation, saying it was the best ride of my trip. He grinned, wished me good luck in his thick accent, and pulled out into traffic.

Walking through the campus toward the Registration building, I had to grin at my appearance. Here I was in heavy coat and clothing, boots, with a knitted cap on my head, backpack on my back, and a guitar in my hand. Several coeds passed me and looked with curiosity. They had on shorts and tank tops. It was warm. I grinned to myself as I walked.

In the Registration office, they told me that most students had not yet returned to campus, as the semester would not begin for a few weeks. Tom's girlfriend was not yet back.

"Great," I replied. I explained that I was trying to find a place to sleep and was a thousand miles from home, with little money. The young woman behind the counter told me I could stay at the guest rooms. She would "sponsor" me for the evening. I thanked her.

"One problem," she said. "The guest lodging is on the other side of the campus, and the front desk closes at three o'clock. That's in ten minutes. You'll have to hurry. I'll call and let them know you are coming."

By this time, two other ladies were standing beside the helpful one. All were smiling. "Good luck," they said.

"Thanks!" I replied, waving, hurrying out the door. In my heavy clothing, tennis shoes dangling on the outside of my backpack, and my sleeping bag roll trying to fall out one side from being tied beneath the backpack, I was running across the campus—laughing at myself, out loud, the entire time! I could only imagine how strange I appeared to these students. The tennis shoes were bouncing up and down, beating against the backpack. I had to switch the guitar from my right to my left hand so I could hold the sleeping bag roll in place with my right hand. With about three minutes to spare, I arrived at the guest quarters.

There were two ladies at the counter. They grinned when they saw me. The woman at the Registration office told them about this strangely dressed guy on his way over, and they had been waiting, perhaps wishing the stranger good luck arriving before the closing time.

I checked in and went to my room. Finally, I could relax.

I had not told my parents or anyone else that I was leaving Virginia Beach. I simply left. Now I needed to let my family know I was okay. My older sister lived in North Carolina. I did not know how to explain to my parents, or what I would try to tell them, so I called my sister. I told her to tell everyone that I was safe and in New Orleans, on my way to Houston. I told her I would be in touch when I got settled there. In the meantime, I did not want anyone to worry.

Upon arriving in Houston, I called Tom Ebner from a gas station. He drove there and picked me up, taking me to the apartment where he and his father lived. Mr. Ebner invited me to stay while I sought work. I was down to thirty dollars. Had they not allowed me to stay, I do not know what I would have done. I would always be grateful to them for their hospitality, as well as to all of the people who took a chance and gave a young stranger a ride when he needed one.

Tom allowed me to use his car to interview at an employment agency. I got a job as a yard hand at a land drilling company. They were based in Conroe, Texas, but their operations yard was in southeast Houston. My job was to help load drilling equipment onto trucks, to be taken to field locations where it would be assembled into a complete drilling rig.

After my second week, I was advised that the trucks would be sent to Victoria, Texas, to pick up major pieces of equipment that were being refurbished there. Tom had told me that drilling crews were often picked up locally when a drilling rig was moved into a new area. I decided to take a chance. I thanked Tom and his father for everything, grabbed my backpack and guitar, and hitchhiked all night to the gates of the drilling company yard. As soon as the first driver arrived and opened the gate, I carried my pack and guitar to the truck to which I was assigned, and stowed them in the back of the cab.

Later, when my truck's driver arrived, I did not say a word to him about the gear. We got into the truck and headed to Victoria. There we loaded the equipment and drove to a farm outside the small Texas town of New Ulm. Assembling the drilling rig took two days, as much fitting work was required to place the new and refurbished equipment into proper places and alignments.

We worked all night the first night. The evening of the second day, I pulled my gear from the truck and placed it behind a tree, out of sight from the drilling location. When I returned to the truck, the driver told me it was time to go back to Houston. I told him to go on back by himself; I was going to try getting onto the drilling crew. He laughed, shook his head, and said he guessed I knew what I was doing. I told him I hoped so. He wished me good luck. We shook hands. He drove away.

The rig foreman, or "toolpusher," had his office in a portable trailer. His name was Tommy. I knocked on the door, walked into Tommy's office, and told him I wanted to train for the drilling crew. I told him I knew nothing about it but was strong, intelligent, and eager to learn. He said, "Fair enough," and told me to be there at 7:00 AM.

I caught a ride into town with two of the men, where we ate, and I bought food for the next day. I slept in the woods. By the time 7:00 AM arrived, I had been up a couple of hours, eager to begin. After several days of training, the personnel were assigned to crews of four or five persons: a driller, a derrickman, and either two or three floormen. I was a floorman, the starting position. I was assigned to the "morning tour" crew, working from 11:00 PM to 7:00 AM.

After work in the morning, I would go into Tommy's trailer and study his books on drilling and the equipment. My college education in physics and engineering drafting enabled me to comprehend how the equipment functioned and how it all worked together to drill holes.

Tommy called me into his office one morning, more than two weeks after I had been there. "You surprised the main office," he stated. "They thought that you had quit when you didn't return with the truck." He grinned at me. "When I sent in your time sheet, they asked how you were working out. I told them you were coming along well and that you should remain here, with the rig."

"Thanks, Tommy," I replied. "You won't regret it."

He reached out his hand. "See you tonight," he said. I shook his hand and left. I'd done it! I'd stowed away on the truck and earned a position on the drill crew!

Throughout 1978, I traveled through much of southeast Texas, working on the drilling rig, following it from one hole location to the next. Having very little money, I initially slept in a tent some distance away from the rig, for several months. The inconvenience of a tent had nothing to do with what I perceived of myself and situation. I started with essentially nothing, trying to earn my way into a future. The drilling rig enabled me to contribute, and through those contributions to earn a living and the benefits of an income. Later, the company bought a sleeping trailer for the employees.

Living beside the rig, in the tent, I had spent many mornings sitting outside the tent, looking at sunlight refract through dew on hillsides. More than once, a cow in the pasture had wandered up to the tent, curious about this "thing" sitting in its grazing area, waking me with a loud moo. There had been many beautiful sunrises and sunsets, and wild bluebonnets waving in the spring breezes. The evening dew would have settled upon the tent by the time I had showered after work. Many days, the sun's glistening light would appear as a blanket on the tent's exterior. My conversations with the cows were generally brief and direct: "Get the hell away."

On days off, a coworker named Bryan and I would go to places in the Texas Hill Country. We would go camping, hiking, and whitewater canoeing. I had gotten into bare-hand rock climbing and cliff diving. I don't know if having been raised with the excitement of competitive sports almost all of my life was the impetus, but I found great enjoyment in pushing myself to overcome challenges. I climbed cliffs just because they were there. I jumped and dived from cliffs for the rush of freefalling toward the water.

Work on the rig was strenuous and dirty. After work, we were frequently covered head-to-toe in drilling fluids, grease, or dry chemicals used to make the drilling fluid. Working on the rig gave a sense of accomplishment, as each well was a separate project, having a start activity and an end result. Not all of the wells had been successful in finding oil or gas, but each was a completed project.

One time, we had been drilling near the town of Sealy, west of Houston, in an open field. I was up in the rig's derrick more than one hundred feet above the ground. This crop-dusting plane was working nearby, and I watched him for a while as he passed back and forth above the fields. I looked down at the work being done on the drilling rig floor. When I next looked to my left for the crop duster, he was headed straight for the derrick! He flew straight at me, veering off to the side at the last minute. I could see the pilot's face just before he turned. That was how close he was! He "buzzed" me four or five times, to his amusement. I wasn't so amused.

There were some great times that year. However, they were also lonely. I missed female companionship, and that of my family. Midway through the year, I decided I wanted to go back to school. I saved money so I could return to college. By December, I had saved well over a thousand dollars.

Early in the second week of December, I had given the company my notice and informed them of my intention of returning to college. They wished me luck and told me I had a job whenever I wanted one. I thanked them all, loaded my gear into an old pickup truck I had purchased, and left the rig with a coworker named Kevin. I called my parents from a gas station on the outskirts of El Campo the next morning and told them I was on my way back, to go back to school. They were excited.

I drove the first day all the way to Mobile, Alabama, where I stayed in a hotel about a half-hour drive north of the city. I called my parents collect to tell them where I was and that I expected to arrive in two more days. I wanted to see some friends in North Carolina on my way through.

Christmas was very merry that year. I would enroll in Old Dominion University, in Norfolk, Virginia, and continue my education in engineering. Until I could get in, I intended to work and continue putting money aside. That all suddenly changed, beginning the morning of December 30.

My youngest sister and I were sitting in the TV room that my father, brothers, and I had converted of the garage. The pre-game show was beginning for the American Football Conference championship game between Denver and the Steelers. My youngest sister, Barbara, and I were nibbling on candy from our Christmas stockings. I was barefoot, in blue jeans and a T-shirt, sitting on the couch.

There was a knock at the front door. My father, who was in the kitchen, walked through the dining room to answer the door. A few moments later, he called to me. "Mike," he said, "There are some gentlemen here who would like to talk to you."

I walked through the kitchen and turned toward the dining room. There stood two Virginia Beach police officers. "Can I help you?" I asked, curious as to why policemen would be asking for me.

"Are you Michael Crabtree?" one asked.

"Yes," I replied.

The larger policeman approached me. "You are under arrest! Face the wall and spread your arms and legs apart!" He grasped one of my arms to turn me. He began reading me my rights. I was astonished! Surely this was a dream, a nightmare. I was being arrested in my home. What was this all about? I had to know, now.

"...court of law. Do you understand your rights as I have read them to you? If not, I will go over them again," the officer said. He was about my height but probably outweighed me by twenty pounds.

"I understand them," I said. "What am I being charged with?" I blurted, my mind searching for a grip on reality.

"Where is the thirty-eight?" the second officer asked.

"Thirty-eight what?" I replied, as handcuffs clamped tightly around my wrists.

"Texas said you have a gun, a thirty-eight revolver."

"If you find it, you can have it," I quipped. "I've never owned a gun, and I don't have one now." My brain still refused to accept the seriousness of the situation.

I paused, looking first at the officers and then at my father. A stunned disbelief was apparent on his face. "What is this about? Why am I being arrested?"

"You are wanted on a fugitive warrant from Texas," answered the shorter, heavier policeman.

"What for?" I asked.

"Aggravated robbery," he said.

"That's crazy! I'd never do anything like that!" I stated emphatically.

"You can tell that to the detectives," replied the taller, leaner policeman. He pulled a radio from a holder on his belt. "Unit 27," he said into the radio.

"Twenty-seven," came the reply.

"Dad," I said, looking straight into my father's eyes. "I honest to God don't know what the hell is going on. I know nothing about this!"

This made absolutely no sense. My father did not reply. His gaze wandered from me to the officers and back. He seemed stupefied, in a trance.

"Suspect apprehended," said the policeman into his radio. "You can pull the car in front of the house."

The heavier policeman grabbed my bare arm. "We're going," he said.

"Wait," I began. "It's cold out there. Could I at least get a coat?"

"Sure," he replied. "Where is it?"

"Dad," I asked, "would you get my coat from the closet?"

"Where is it?" he softly replied.

"It's there, in the closet," I said, nodding at the dining room closet doors, unable to point with my hands.

My father took out the coat and draped it over my shoulders. His silence ended and a barrage of questions poured rapidly from his mouth, none of which registered in my awareness. My mind was a blur.

The officer again grasped my arm, slightly pulling it in a gesture to begin walking to the front door. The lean officer opened the door. As I approached it, a motion at the top of the stairs caught my attention. The door was at the landing of the stairs leading to the upper floor. At the top was my mother. I stopped.

"Mom," I said almost pleadingly, "I don't know what's going on."

"Let's go," the officer stated, pushing against my arm.

As the cold air hit my face, my eyes watered. The sun was bright, the air dry. A sky blue police car was approaching the house from the cul-de-sac. My bare feet fell into place walking down the driveway. In my mental state of confusion, I had not thought to ask for shoes. Although cold, the driveway was dry, rough cement. It was not painful. An officer appeared at the corner of the house, holstering his service revolver. *I must be dangerous,* I thought. Why else would they pull the car around the corner and approach the house on foot? The car stopped. The lean officer opened the door. Another officer was walking around my 1962 Chevy pickup truck, parked in the driveway.

"Have you radioed in?" asked the lean officer.

"Yes," the third one replied. "A tow truck is being dispatched from the garage. I'll stay here until it arrives."

Mike Haskett, a friend I had known for years, had stopped his truck on the opposite side of the driveway from the police car. He had come to watch the game with my family. He was beside his truck as I walked down the driveway. He had waited until I passed and then walked up the driveway.

The heavy one turned me, my back to the open door, and placed a hand on my head. Before being seated in the car, I looked to the house. My father was standing outside the front door, and my mother was looking through the window of the outer storm door. Barbara was crying, standing on the porch. They did not wave, just watched—dumbfounded—as I sat down and turned my legs forward. The car door shut.

The heavy officer walked in front of the car and got into the front passenger seat. The slimmer one had walked past the car, toward the cul-de-sac, where a second car had appeared.

"Are the cuffs too tight?" the officer asked, his voice sounding sincere.

"No, they're okay," I replied, understanding that these men were just doing their jobs.

I looked at the officer as he lifted the microphone from its clasp. He was a light haired man of about thirty. He called in, notifying the dispatcher that we were on our way. The car pulled away from the curb.

"How did they identify me?" I asked, trying to begin making sense of what was occurring.

"Your truck," replied the officer who was driving. "It was the one used in the robbery."

That answer was of no immediate help. I had resolved myself to the fact that I had been arrested for something I had never done. Or, had I in some unknowing way been a victim of trusting gullibility? I had no idea when or where the crime occurred, so I temporarily stopped searching through memories looking for clues. This was going to require more evidence through which to sort.

The ride was not uncomfortable as I was driven, stunned, through the area that had shaped and molded me. I was physically present in the car, but my mind had raced far ahead, preparing for what lie ahead at the police station. I momentarily rejoined my arresters when they began cursing at a few juveniles riding their bikes on a narrow road, but for the rest of the ride I sat staring dumbly into space.

The police took me through a service entrance in the back of the station, to the detective bureau on the second floor. I was searched again, after being led into a small room with an old, marred wooden table and two chairs. The only other door in the room led to a very clean restroom with no windows or other doors. The room was uncomfortably quiet, so I hummed and sang to myself until the door opened and two casually dressed men entered.

"I'm Detective Keller," one said, a Mediterranean-looking man in his mid-thirties, with very dark, straight hair and a five o'clock shadow, although it was apparent that he had shaved. He was not intimidating in motion or inflection, and the defenses that I had erected when the doorknob turned weakened. "And this is Detective Newby," he said. A round-faced man with thick, light-brown hair and a multi-colored mustache nodded in acknowledgment.

"We have been handling your case," Keller continued. "Did they read you your rights when you were arrested?"

"Yes, they did," I answered.

"Well, here is a written copy, with a place for a written statement if you wish to waive your rights and make one," Keller said.

He handed me a sheet of paper with a copy of the Miranda rights upon arrest. I was familiar with the case from high school. There was a line for a signature, indicating that one understood the document but would waive the right to silence and make a statement. I signed the paper and wrote that I had no knowledge of any armed robbery in Texas, that I had at no time possessed a handgun of any description, and that two coworkers—Kevin Silver and Ernie Thompson—had also used my truck while I was in Texas.

"When did the crime occur?" I questioned, trying to begin defending myself.

"Texas didn't say," Keller responded. "I talked to a Captain Brooks, and he said that he did not have all of the information at hand, presently."

Keller began asking questions about my possible involvement. He said that the truck had been identified by the license plate. I told him that the arrest was a shock to me and that the act of robbery was so much against my nature as to be absurd.

Newby interrupted, concerning the truck, stepping away from the exit door and closing the gap between us. He asked about the general description and then mentioned the headlights being out of alignment.

"Mine were fine," I emphasized, seeing a detail which I could use to the affirmative. "But they may have been dirty at the time."

"What do you mean by 'at the time'?" Newby spoke aggressively, leaning slightly closer to me.

Realizing the mistake I had made, I fumbled for the right words to explain my thinking. The surprise of his aggression caused my eyes to widen and my face to redden.

"Oh, when Keller said the truck identification was positive by the tags, I assumed it *was* my truck. When the crime was committed, the headlights may have been covered by the dirt from the muddy roads back to the rig."

They understood my reasoning and the response that I gave, which was a great relief to me. From then on, the questioning was about the possible involvement of Kevin Silver or Ernie Thompson in the crime. I explained that because a blowout of an oil rig can occur at any time, and anything within fifty yards would be melted or scorched by the heat, I left the keys in the ignition at all times.

"They could use the truck whenever they needed it," I said.

"Did either one of them have a grudge against you or want to frame you for any reason?" Keller asked, opening another area to be explored.

"Yes," I quickly replied. "Kevin had a girlfriend, Sally. They had been living together. She left him. She moved out of his apartment, and I started seeing her," I told them. "I invited her to a pool party at my apartment complex, and word got back to Kevin. Kevin got drunk one night and challenged me to a fight.

"We did not fight that night or any night," I told Keller. "She got bored with me after awhile, and ran off with another friend of mine. Kevin and I got over it, I thought, but maybe he really didn't." I found myself building an incriminating case against Kevin, in self-defense. The story sounded convincing, and I realized I was taking cheap shots at someone, ignorant of his innocence or guilt. I was fighting a possible prison sentence with nothing but my tongue.

The questioning went on for another thirty minutes before the two detectives left. My father came in for a few minutes, and we talked. He was unable to add anything to what I knew.

A different police officer came into the room. I was led downstairs, to a van that took me to the magistrate's office. There, I was informed that I would remain in jail until court opened on January 2, for my extradition hearing.

Great, I thought. *New Year's in jail!*

Cement Walls and Metal Nets

The cement wall was cold through my T-shirt as I sat in the cloud of my cigarette's smoke, looking at the bars that caged me. There was no telling what time it was, because there was no day or night in this fluorescent world of walls and bars. Disbelief was all I could muster. For all of my failures and mistakes, robbery was completely out of character for me.

I knew nothing of an armed robbery in Weimar, Texas, where Keller had said it occurred. How was I to prove it?

My mind wandered, retrieving a mental picture of Anna, whom I had met in the spring of my freshman year at NC State. I thought back to my involvement with her, my hopes and plans, and the suffering she had caused me. She had not meant to, but it must have been difficult being in love with two people. I had forgiven her for living a lie through my next year and a half in college and out. I had wanted to marry her, not knowing the entire truth. Her letter, received two days before Christmas a year ago, gave me no indication why she was calling everything off and could no longer speak to me or see me.

Between my depression over my job situation, Anna, and one of my roommates beating his girlfriend in our three-bedroom apartment, I could not sleep or eat. I felt like I was about to emotionally snap. In mid-January, I had packed my backpack, grabbed my guitar, and hit the road in search of myself. Tom Ebner had said there was work in Texas.

On my way through Burlington, North Carolina, the third day, I tried calling Anna. She lived in Burlington. I had eaten at a fast food restaurant that had a pay phone outside. My intention was to find out if I had done something wrong when Anna had visited me in Virginia, in November. The afternoon air was cool, but not uncomfortable, although the wind was chilling my face. The sun was bright in a pretty much cloudless sky.

Her mother answered the telephone. I had not met or previously talked with her mother, so I introduced myself. "Oh, Anna has told me so much about you."

"Mrs. Williams, I was on my way through town and was hoping I'd get a chance to talk to Anna," I replied.

"She isn't here, at the moment," her mother explained. "Does that mean you're not going to be here for the wedding?"

"No, ma'am," I said, stunned. My blood fell to my feet, and I started shaking. "When is the wedding?"

"She and Keith set it for two weeks from Saturday."

"Tell her I wish her the best, but unfortunately I can't make the wedding." I stared at the telephone receiver in my hand, pausing a moment before again speaking. "Mrs. Williams, I need to get going. It was nice talking to you."

"I'll tell Anna that you called," she said.

I thanked her and hung up. Anna had always told me Keith was her cousin, although in the back of my mind I had at times wondered.

Hearing this news on the third day of my journey dispelled any thoughts I had entertained about returning home in the near future. I became determined to make it to Houston and begin anew. Now, in my prison cell, I thought about the six-day trip, remembering my run through Tulane University and the looks on the faces of the coeds. I laughed, and it echoed off the cement walls.

The year had produced some of the best—and loneliest—times in my life. My constantly traveling with the rig left little time to make friends other than my coworkers. Sitting in my prison cell, I wondered how my friends would take the news of my arrest on a fugitive warrant for armed robbery. Surely they could not think I would do such a thing?

Footsteps pierced my train of thought, and I looked up to find a trustee bringing my dinner. "Here ya go, my man," he said, placing the tray on the little shelf below the small opening between the door bars.

"It doesn't look too bad," I offered, hoping to talk with him. I rose from the bunk—a metal frame protruding from the wall, with a lumpy gray mattress on it—threw my half-smoked cigarette into the toilet intruding from the back wall of my little cell, and walked toward him.

"It's not too bad tonight," he said with a grin as he turned to leave. No more conversation was offered on his part, and I was so new to this environment I felt it best to just leave it at that. I was very hungry, not having eaten before or since my arrest that morning. The food was gone before my appetite. He was right: it wasn't too bad, if you like cold food.

I drifted in and out of sleep for quite a while, having no way of telling how long. Each time I awoke with the word "Weimar" on my tongue. "When the hell were you ever in Weimar, Texas?" I would ask myself aloud, since no one else could hear. The same answer kept coming back from within: *I can't remember!* There were so many small towns I'd drifted through while working on the rig, and although I usually remembered the location of each one, if nothing else about it, I could not sort Weimar out from the list. I had heard of it, but to my knowledge had never been there or to the curbside store I was supposed to have robbed.

The Virginia Beach police arrested me on a fugitive warrant, telling me I was wanted for armed robbery. My truck had been positively identified by the license plates. I did not remember Weimar... and the magistrate said Texas wanted me held without bail, but that one could be set at fifty thousand dollars if I pushed the matter. My parents would pay a bondsman, I knew, but would be giving away the money, never to see it again. I had agreed to no bail for that reason. I had always wondered what being behind bars would be like, as an experience, but now—I chuckled to myself—I was getting far more experience than I had wanted.

When I next woke, the guard was locking a verbal and obviously intoxicated slender young man in the cell next to mine. He was slurring and, after the guard left, was determined that I would be a good audience for his complaints. I listened for a while but grew tired, with boredom if nothing else.

The light in the hall had been turned off, so I assumed it must be near midnight. Another hall-mate had been compelled to join the slender guy and me: a black man, I would guess from the voice. He was unmoved by my next-door-neighbor's story, being busy trying to coax the guard into calling the bondsman again.

I finally manipulated the complainer into ending his story and being quiet, and I closed my eyes. I woke to a peculiar sound similar to wheels on little rolling service carts, like those in hospitals. The smell of sausage filled the corridor.

Perhaps unconsciously, the position I had taken in preparing to sleep was with my feet in the direction of the hall from which most traffic seemed to originate, so my field of vision was of people approaching in the hallway. Hearing the service cart, I rolled to the left and sat up, opening my eyes. The trustee placed my breakfast on its shelf in the door.

"What time is it?" I asked, wiping sleep from my eye.

"It's about 6:30," he replied.

He turned to my skinny hall-mate and became consumed in conversation. I was listening so attentively I was unaware a second trustee had arrived.

"Coffee?" he asked, holding an aluminum pitcher.

"Yes, please," I replied, rising to my feet.

I could not remember my neighbor's face, as I was only partially awake when he was brought past my cell the previous night. All that I could see from my bars was a bearded trustee talking to a pair of thin arms. The trustee was being asked about some of the more senior inmates. I found it fascinating that the skinny fellow's concern for the senior inmates was genuine, and then realized that a human being needs contact with others, regardless of the environment.

I was hungry until I saw breakfast. It would have been very good if the eggs and link sausage were not half-submersed in solid grease. Scraping was to little avail. It removed most of the grease, but I was barely able to stomach the bits I could not scrape off. A sip of coffee every three bites burned my mouth but settled my queasiness.

"Oh my gosh," I said in amazement as I reached for a cigarette.

"What is it?" my neighbor asked.

"I smoked two packs in half a day yesterday."

"That's not hard to do in here," said a third voice, two cells to my left, on the other side of my skinny neighbor.

"That's the truth," came from next door, in a voice that even *sounded* skinny.

I tried to picture the fellow next door, as we began talking about our cases and ourselves. I was interested in their stories, which seemed to me odd. I knew I was innocent and these two were not. When my turn came, my story spilled like groceries from a torn bag. My mind was trying to clear itself of the tremendous store of thoughts and pictures it had been commanded to ingest the previous day.

My father had been able to see me in the detective's office before I was jailed. He said he had talked to someone named Captain Brooks, who did not know much about the investigation.

"When did the crime occur?" I impatiently asked, waiting for something to begin jarring my memory.

"He said it was about a week before you left Texas," Dad replied, trying to sound unshaken by that bit of information. It looked as though I would have some explaining to do when I got back to Texas. My father asked if I had loaned my truck to anyone that week.

"Yes, I did," I remembered, having thought over the two months that I had owned it. Anyone at the rig could have used it. I tried to remember when Kevin and Ernie may have used the truck the week before I left Texas. I knew the crime was committed during the evening, and before 10:30 PM, because an eyewitness had noticed the left headlight was misaligned. That meant that it had to have been after sunset, and before 10:30 PM, because that was when we were always at the rig, to report to work by 11:00 PM. We all stayed in the bunkhouse at the rig, and as far as I knew all used the truck to get food, but before 10:30.

I had been eating in one of three towns the entire week: Eagle Lake, Columbus, or Altair, all of which were within fifteen miles of the rig. I could not see how they could place me in a store in Weimar that week. That could have been my truck, but perhaps not necessarily the one.

I did not think Ernie would rob a store, but I had reservations about Kevin. He had a devil-may-care attitude about many things.

My fellow inmates had been listening to me ramble for quite a while. Finally, I finished. It was a relief to have gotten it off my mind and chest. I had only touched the surface of the pool of memories I had recalled, having gone over the last week in Texas countless times, probably twice for each cigarette.

My mind had replayed the entire week as though a television movie in parts except, in my excited state, there was no chronology, only associations back and forth in time. Faces, places, conversations, and even emotions came to mind. I knew I was innocent, and my mind was being squeezed for every moment stored within to prove it. I lit a cigarette, already having a veritable fleet of butts floating in the toilet.

"You should have no trouble beating that," piped the guy next door, breaking the momentary silence that filled our confines.

"Yeah, no trouble at all," came the other voice. "You sure did get a bum deal."

Nothing more was said. After finishing the cigarette, I took the clothes off I'd been wearing since the previous morning, and laid down to rest. I was on the verge of sleep's respite from thought when the guards stopped at my cell.

"Crabtree, get up and put on your clothes," blared the stout, middle-aged sergeant. "You have a visitor."

Visiting hours for letters A—M had been the previous afternoon, so I could not figure out who it was. We turned to the lobby by the booking department, waited for a bar door to open, and went toward the Visiting Room. The security control room of this new, multimillion dollar prison, on the same hall, was filled with closed circuit television pictures of the halls and even some cells in the three-story jail. The guard unlocked the heavy metal door to the Visiting Room and I entered.

No one else was in the cement-walled room. It was a dull, semi-gloss green, almost an unripe apple color. There were three small divisions of a long table-like shelf, with a partition between each little booth. There was a single chair for each, facing the large windows reinforced with steel mesh of thin wire. Through the window on the right I could see the one man who I did not want to know anything of my arrest, but I smiled as we both approached the window.

"Hello, Father," I said with great humility.

"Hello, Mike. How are your spirits?" he inquired over the telephone linking us.

"They're okay. I have trusted the system so far. I know I am innocent, but they don't," I told him.

Father French had known me for more than six years, from the first masses we celebrated as a new parish. I was fifteen then. Over the next three years, he and my fellow parishioners treated me almost as an adult. By the time I was eighteen, I had been nominated to the parish council. Two years later, I was involved in study to become a Catholic priest, but circumstantial changes with my attending college occurred. My zeal for the faith had diminished greatly. This man had seen me as a good albeit adventurous and perhaps impulsive Christian young man, but my eyes had lost their teenage innocence, and he was more than just conscious of it. He was seeing me at my most humbled hour: no strength, no zeal, only trust.

"I have to play this by the system's rules and trust that the truth will win," I told him.

"And if it doesn't. . . ?" he queried, probing to see if I was prepared for the cruelty that life's cards sometimes deal.

"Then I'll confront that situation when I come to it," I replied, aware of the five years to life that accompanies an armed robbery conviction in Texas, but not wanting to give conviction a second thought.

Perhaps it was a feeling of helplessness more than anything else, but my nerves were fine. In fact, perhaps self-deluded, I felt as though I controlled the situation. My tone had become very matter-of-fact as we talked for a few more minutes.

Father French walked out the front door as I walked through one through which you could see, but enclosed you all the same. It was like being in a metal net.

My hall-mates' questioning was not really annoying, because I was now part of their captivity, as they were part of mine. It did not last long as I did not have anything to add to what I had told them earlier. We could hear a television playing somewhere nearby, so we quieted down and tried to listen to the football game: Houston versus Miami.

My eyes opened to the distinct sound of plastic on metal. The trustee had served us last this evening, New Year's Eve. The city had graciously given each of us slices of roast beef with gravy—quite a bit better than the fish sandwich that had been offered for lunch. Orange drink was still our mealtime beverage.

"I sure wish this was a beer," I said between sips.

"You and me both," came from the second cell down.

"This isn't quite what I had in mind for New Year's Eve," I said, reflecting on the parties I had been invited to attend that evening.

The food tray never seemed to hold as much as a stomach, and I quickly stripped it bare. It was by far the best food I had had in my short stay, but it left me hungry before it could satiate my appetite. Sometimes tasting something good in a limited quantity was worse than not having had anything. A match lit and nicotine was dessert.

Weimar still made no sense. The missing piece in this enigma was the exact date, but I had eliminated every day that I had been in Texas during December. Yet there had to be something I'd overlooked. Why else would the police have such a good case against me?

Freedom: that was quite a concept. It was something I had never questioned in my ability to make decisions. The only decisions I could make in this eight-foot square cubicle were on which side to sleep, when I would flush the cigarette butts down the drain, and when I would use the toilet for its intended purpose. There was really no deciding even these trivial matters. I slept in whatever position I happened to assume, pushed the lever down when the cigarette butts became a distraction from boredom, and the natural necessity could be delayed only so long.

"Mike, you awake?" came the voice of my skinny hall-mate.

"Yeah, I'm up," I said grumpily, not toward him but at the entire situation.

"How long I been sleepin'?" he asked, audibly yawning as he spoke.

"I don't know. Probably a couple of hours."

"Whatcha been thinking about?" he asked.

"Oh, about my case," I hesitatingly responded.

"It must be a bad feeling to know you're in here and you're innocent," he sympathized.

"Yeah, it's ..." I did not finish. When I felt ready to break the silence, I heard footsteps approaching.

"Happy New Year," the heavy, gray-haired man said affectedly as he walked briskly by our cells.

After the footstep sounds ceased, I began to loudly laugh. My slender companion did not comprehend what had just happened.

"Who was that?" he asked. "Do you know him?"

"That was Sheriff Smith," I chuckled.

"Well, what's so funny?"

"I've known him for more than five years, and I never thought I'd ever be under this division of his departments," I explained.

Skinny chuckled a few times.

"Happy New Year," I softly said, realizing the good time I was missing outside of the walls.

"Happy New Year," replied my hall-mates.

"It can't get any worse. It can only get better," I offered.

"Let's hope so," we all echoed.

"Happy New Year!" I yelled.

Skinny yelled next. We yelled "Happy New Year" for what seemed ten or fifteen minutes, until our enthusiasm slowed to a trickle. It had become very quiet, and I was preparing to go to sleep when all hell broke loose on the floors above us.

"What's that?" I asked.

"It's New Year's!" Skinny yelled, running his plastic cup across the bars of his cell. "They are probably watching the shows on TV."

"Happy New Year!" beamed my other neighbor's voice, accompanied by the sound of his toilet flushing.

"Happy New Year!" I screamed at the top of my lungs, pushing down the handle on my toilet.

Skinny must have been stomping or jumping on his bunk, judging from the next-door noise. "Happy New Year!" he hollered.

We yelled and stomped and flushed and banged until we could no longer. It was as though we were trying to convince ourselves of our exclamations' truth.

The balloon of my anger and frustration burst, spouting "Happy New Year" and laughs of desperation. I had been able to keep from losing my composure to this point, but my rattling of the cell door became as much an angry protest as a celebration. The balloon became pieces and air, and I settled and surrendered to sleep.

The next day, convinced that anything was better than boredom, I began exercising until I broke a sweat. Skinny heard me and started his own workout. That didn't last long.

Sleep had become like elevator doors, opening to things outside the cell. I was tremendously enjoying a dream on one floor when the trustee woke me for lunch. It seemed that the kitchen would never run out of orange drink. Lunch was quickly gone. Pretending that the fish sandwich was something else didn't change its taste, but it occurred to me that my imagination might get an extended period of exercise if I could not come up with answers.

"So this is 1979. What a way to start," I mumbled under my breath. My family would be slow in waking this morning. So would Karen. Their concern for me brought tears.

"Everyone believes so much in me, but they don't see why I've done what I have for the past year," I whispered to myself. "How can I ever explain the changes I've seen?"

They could not see the disillusion and distaste ensuing from what had transpired. What had begun as competition with myself for situational personal accomplishment had ended in self-rejection and a sense of emptiness. The façade of social importance was thin. The goal of accomplishment that had made me a hero from my athletic abilities had made me compromise my most important values.

My mind wandered back to the disappointing events that so changed my life. After my injury at NC State, I had requested to sit out the rest of the season, to heal. Coach Rein said I was a starter on the football team and had to continue playing. Physical therapy took two and a half hours each day, in addition to practices and weight lifting, films, plus missed class times due to physician appointments. My electrical engineering studies were interrupted for the benefit of the football team.

I had to drop mandatory engineering classes after having been awarded an All-Conference Academic Excellence award the prior year, because I was too far behind to catch up. As a result, I had to change my major to physics and mathematics and had to go to summer school to remain academically eligible to play football the following fall, just to remain in school.

At the end of the spring training season, the professional football scouts came to the campus to scout players. After running a couple of laps around the training track, we were grouped to be timed in the forty yard dash. Among the quickest on the team, I had been selected to run with one of the team's promising juniors. I was not yet warmed up sufficiently, continuing to stretch my legs up to the moment we had to run. Three steps from the finish I felt a pull in the top of my thigh, followed by pain. I had pulled a quadriceps muscle in my right thigh.

Two days later, we were expected to lift weights to our maximum lift capacity. I had done all of the lifts except the squat, in which the weight bar was held across the top of the shoulders and the lifter slowly bends the knees, lowering the weight. When the legs reached a half-bent position, the lifter then reverses, lifting the weight in returning to a standing position. All of the weight was borne by the thighs. My right thigh was heavily taped, and it ached. The defensive line coach was in charge of the squat lifts. I told him I had a muscle pull and would probably worsen it by trying the lift. He said, "No excuses—get after it." I did as he said, worsening the injury.

Instead of playing football so that I could get an engineering education, I was going to school to play football. Classes and study had become second in importance. Under Coach Holtz, education was first. Apparently not so under Coach Rein, who had something to prove for his own reasons. I felt betrayed. I'd gone from being an honors student in engineering to mandatorily attending summer school in order to remain academically eligible to play and so remain in college.

Everyone was shocked that I left college and football. The coaching staff released to the press that I had left to enter the seminary and become a priest. That was convenient for them. Although studying to be a priest, through a series of weekend seminars held by the Diocese of Richmond, my relationship with Anna was making me uncertain, and I had theological difficulties with some of the Church's teachings.

It was difficult to make people understand that ultimately, football was a game played by athletes, sportswriters, those who appreciated the skill, and those who wished they could have been in the spotlight of notoriety. It was entertainment: a game. A few years of notoriety weren't worth the rest of a lifetime of physical impairment to me, especially as academics had been relegated to secondary status by the coaching staff. I told Coach Rein I did not want to continue playing.

Occasionally, someone would side with me and replenish my faith in the decision I had made. Most, however, did not understand.

Having left college, I returned to work in the shipyards in Norfolk, where I had worked summers as a rigger. It was there that I started smoking cigarettes. In August, with a slowdown in ship repair activity, I was laid off.

Anna came to see me in early November, as we'd been in contact frequently after my departure from college. Plans had formulated in my mind. It would be rough at first, but I planned to work while she finished her final year of college, after which I would return to school. I remembered seeing her for the first time in months, when she drove to Virginia Beach in November. The day was …

My daydream was interrupted by the guard. "You have a visitor."

"I didn't think I could have any except on Saturday," I replied.

"Today is New Year's. Visitors are allowed on holidays," he said.

I put on my T-shirt, and we left. The guard opened the door to the Visiting Room. There stood Karen outside the glass window. She looked beautiful as always, her reddish brown hair falling gently over her sweater, her hazel eyes bright and penetrating. She had waited for so long for me to decide if I wanted our futures to merge. She would wait no longer. I could not blame her, but my feelings for her had always been confusing.

Our pasts coincided back through college and high school. Her beauty was a complex mixture of woman and child. To those around her she was a person of drive, determination, compassion, and self-certainty. Her family was prominent in the area, a few generations past, and she carried herself with a self-assurance, as though royalty. She had had a rough teenage period, and there was an underlying insecurity she did not let anyone else see.

She had always attracted me, at one point many years previous having told her I loved her. I did love her, but something in her brought cautiousness to my actions. Something about her always weakened me, many times to the point of despising the vulnerability I felt in her presence. She was so damned certain. She knew what she wanted, unquestioningly. That was frightening.

We had talked of her coming to live with me in Texas back in June. I had visited Virginia Beach for the first time since leaving in January and contacted her. We saw each other almost every day during my visit, and for the first time in our six year relationship, we became lovers. She was so passionate, so trusting. It heightened our feelings: her surety in me and my indecisiveness about her. She could be so domineering, yet so tender and vulnerable.

Returning to Texas, I had written Karen a letter, asking her to come and live with me in Texas. I did not send it. What kind of existence would that have been for her, seeing me only on my two days off, after having worked six consecutive days away at the drilling site?

I just wasn't sure about my feelings. When I was around her she captivated me, but she also seemed to influence my thinking, overpowering it. Part of me had hoped she would become angry with me and decide to end it, but that was not the case.

Having been seeing Karen after arriving in Virginia Beach in December, I sent her the saved Texas letter of June, in my Christmas card to her. Our talk, just before my arrest, was now about marriage. She had initiated the idea, and I had not as yet objected to it. Deep in my heart I knew it was a possibility that would now come to a decision. Her determination made my uncertainty more important to me.

She was smiling through the glass, seemingly oblivious to my being paraded in handcuffs to this meeting. Her voice was cheerful, making me realize how distant the glass divider really made us. She tried to cheer me up, without any real progress. I was glad she was there, but the humiliation of my position permeated my perception of these moments. Her talk of our lives together seemed so ridiculous from my side of the wall. Two weeks ahead was farther than I could see, let alone years, as she was talking.

"Do you want me to come to court tomorrow?" she asked.

"Yes, please," I replied, sincerely wanting her support at the extradition hearing.

"Okay. I'll be there."

I looked past her at the approach of familiar figures. The strain of the arrest and incarceration was a visible burden circling my parents' eyes. They tried to feign cheerfulness, my mother unconsciously biting her lower lip. Her look at me was as though I had a dangerous weight tethered perilously above my head.

Karen turned, noticing my staring past her. "I'll be back," she said, then vacated the seat and moved to a chair near the far wall. She sat self-consciously, trying to interpret my facial expressions. My parents had always liked her but felt that any relationship between us was ill-fated.

My mother sat in front of me, picking up the telephone. "We could not find out much about the case," she began, sighing with open desperation.

Dad picked up the phone in the next window so that they could both speak and listen at the same time. I picked up the phone in the next window. "It looks as though your truck, and possibly you, were involved in that robbery," my father admitted, "at least from what that Captain Brooks said."

"He said your truck was identified by the tags," interjected Mom. She seemed moments away from crying, as tears were welling in her eyes.

"I've been through every minute of my last week in Texas, and all I can come up with is a headache," I told them. "I even wake up thinking of the name 'Weimar,' but I can't place it. As far as I know, I've never been there."

"Well," Mom quickly said, "it looks as though your truck was there."

"What about this Silver fellow?" Dad asked.

"As far as I can tell, the only night that week that we rode together was Saturday, the 9th of December. He and I left the rig, got something to eat, and intended to go to Mexico for a day or so before I left for Virginia."

"Did you pass through any small towns on the way?" Mom asked.

"Yeah, but not Weimar," I answered. "We got stopped in El Campo that evening, because the truck had a taillight out. The policeman searched the truck. That took some time. I had to pay a thirty dollar fine. We changed our plans as a result. We stayed overnight in a hotel there. I called you from El Campo the next morning, and we went on to Houston."

"There must have been some other time that you don't remember," Mom said emphatically, her anxiety apparent.

"Mom, all that week I went to Eagle Lake, Altair, and Columbus, by myself."

"Could Silver have set you up?" Dad asked.

I ran quickly through my prosecution of Kevin. It was ruthless and convincing of necessity. I'd not taken any part in a robbery, and my mind grasped at anything to explain away the implication. There was only one night that Kevin drove my truck in the last week before I left Texas, and my hopes rode flimsily on that fact.

"What other information did you get out of Brooks?" I asked.

"Not much," Dad replied. "He said that he did not know much about the investigation."

"Well," I sighed, "I guess all you can do is keep trying. I've got to have some more answers before my questions make any sense."

"We got hold of a lawyer," my mother interrupted. "He was referred to us by a friend of Father French in Houston. His name is Steve Paris."

"This whole thing is crazy, but it's real!" I loudly exclaimed. "I can't believe it!"

"Mike." My mother stopped my eruption. "I just want you to know that your father and I have talked some things over, and whatever you and Karen decide to do is fine with us. We only want you to be happy."

"Thanks, Mom," I said. "I don't really know what we're going to do yet. We can't consider any future at the moment, but thank you for understanding."

"We've decided that we're going to go ahead with plans for our twenty-fifth wedding anniversary celebration, at the church, tomorrow night," Mom stated. "With all of the planning and effort that everyone has done for it, it wouldn't be right to cancel it because of this."

"I wouldn't want you to, Mom," I replied. "This will be over soon, and your anniversary happens only once."

"Do you want us to be in court tomorrow?" Dad asked.

"Yes! Please!" I emphatically replied, the vehemence with which it came out surprising me.

The three of us knew the situation's gravity. My parents trusted my story and tried to mesh it with that of Captain Brooks. The integrity of the police, I'd been taught, was not usually questioned, and the contraposition of the two tales strained the trust my parents had in me and caused me to beat my brain for an explanation not filed in memory.

I was holding humbly to these two people who, despite my failings and confusion, had steadfastly cushioned my falls with sincerity and honesty. Like a child entangled in a web over which it has no control, I was grasping for strength, guidance, and wisdom gained through living: my parents. We were all aware of my needs. They were wrinkled into my face. Silence swelled from the glass partition, crowding out my further words. The tear that welled in my mother's eye ran down her cheek.

"You know we'll be there if you want us," she offered, as she had for countless problems as far back as I could remember.

Anguish flushed my face and wet my eyes. They had always been there. "I do," freed itself from within me.

"Everything will be all right," Dad said. "We'll see you in the morning."

"We'll go on and let you talk to Karen." Mom sighed, wiping the wetness from her cheek. Tears were just thoughts away for us both.

"Tell everyone I'm okay, will you?"

She nodded, again biting her lip. "We love and trust you," she added.

"I know ..." was all I managed to say, emotions expanding, screaming for release from suppression. "I love you, too," I quietly said in exasperation.

With a "goodbye, hon," my mother hung up and rose, turning toward the exit. My father hung up and turned in unison with her.

They walked over to Karen, and after exchanging pleasantries with her, continued their walk to the front desk in the main lobby.

Karen nervously resumed her place at the partition. "Look, I'll be there if you still want me to," she said, inferring influence by my mother.

"Yes, I still want you there," I loudly responded.

"I have to be going," Karen said, rising to her feet. "Michael, I love you," she said, spreading her hand upon the transparent barrier. Her words, poignant and open, reached my ears phonetically, slowed in time by the importance of their existence.

I opened my mouth without conscious control. Nothing had been prepared to send out of it. My eyes met hers and my silence ended. "I know ..." squeaked out. Her expression remained unaltered. "It's just that I'm not sure. We can't really talk about the future at the moment anyway."

"Yes, we can," she quickly and emphatically replied. "This will be over soon, and you will know how you feel."

The quickness and certitude of her response punctured my composure, and I uttered, "I love you, Karen." I was stunned by my statement, completely ill at ease with what came from my lips but unable to retrieve it. *Is it a step forward?* I asked myself.

Her smile washed me of further thoughts. "Goodbye, dear," she said, once more spreading her palm on the glass barrier.

"See you tomorrow," I said, rising from my chair.

We turned, she toward the main lobby and I toward the metal door. The guard answered my knocks, and as I passed the glass partition through which one could see the main lobby, I saw my parents at the desk, still conversing with the receptionist. We waved to each other as I passed, my wave limited by the handcuffs constraining my wrists, and I was once again filled with humility.

The light numbed with the coldness of reality. The slap of my bare feet on the floor echoed off the hard walls, reminding me of the position I found myself in. Despair chilled me to the bone as I looked at the present and future, clouded by complex, opaque, unanswered questions. My echoing footsteps chased me down the hall into my cell.

The cubicle welcomed me with the loud click of the door closing behind me. Soon, the hum of electrical transformers in the fluorescent light fixtures became audible. I lit a cigarette, sat down, and leaned back against the wall in silence. My mind wandered to possible futures.

"Who came to see you?" Skinny asked.

"My parents and my girlfriend," I curtly replied, not wanting to talk about it. He apparently got the message as he asked no other questions.

Later that day, I was moved to the third floor. They issued me a drab gray jumpsuit and a pair of plastic sandals. These were the standard issue to prisoners not being held in the holding cells on the first floor. I did not really notice the face of the guard who escorted me to the elevator, just the badge and the gun. The rapidity of changes occurring around and to me confused and frightened me. I was dazed. The entire elevator ride up was a blank mental screen pasted over with my father's bewildered look as the handcuffs were first being put on me in his house. His eyes still stared through me in disbelief.

My feet followed the guard down a corridor after we left the elevator. We came to a halt in front of a maze of bars, and the officer opened a panel on the wall. Ahead of us, past two doors of bars, the corridor continued, enclosing caged men.

"Everyone in your cells," bellowed the guard. A second guard came from behind us and assumed a position next to the panel. The first guard flipped a switch and the bars began to slide within the cage. Each individual entered a cell. When all of the men were inside, the guard flipped more switches, closing all bar doors in the cell block, with one exception. He opened the door to the corridor and then the one to the cage. When the second guard escorted me into the cell block, the first guard closed the bar door behind us. I walked without comment to my cell and sat down on the mattress.

With an electric hum, the cell door slid shut and latched with a thud. The cell block door was opened and the officer left. With a similar hum the cell block door closed behind him, as did the door in the corridor. The guard threw a final switch and all of the cell doors opened.

A card game was resumed, as though the past several minutes had been a commonplace occurrence. The players slammed the cards one atop the other as they were being played. The aggressive competitiveness was almost palpable. I turned to the TV for escape, trying to focus on the New Year's Day bowl game. The sensation of studying eyes pricked at my neck.

"What you in for?" queried a rough-voiced black man.

I was intimidated but did not want it to be apparent. The man was much older and bigger than me. "Fugitive warrant," I replied, annoyed.

"What's the charge?"

I looked straight into his eyes. "Armed robbery," I gruffly stated, and then returned to watching the television. There was silence, and the studying ceased. It was not until I was in my cell with the door closed that I felt safe.

It did not seem long before a yelling guard woke me as he passed down the corridor. It was morning, the day of the extradition hearing. Breakfast was tasteless at best, but I ate everything given.

I took part in a card game of spades, surprising myself by the vehemence with which I was alternatively pouncing or defending my position, slapping cards on the table. My hand was played with determination, trying to vindicate a shattered ego, and it seemed every play was critical. The game was interrupted by the guard who woke the cell block.

"The two going to court, you have half an hour to get ready," he loudly announced.

"That's me," I stated to the others playing cards. "Anyone want in?" I gave the cards to a dark haired fellow and walked from the table.

I went to the shower, which was cold, brushed my teeth with a complimentary toothbrush from the city, and shaved with a very-used disposable razor. The same gray uniform awaited my return to the cell, and I could not deny it the outing.

Karen would be there. So would my parents. They had not yet seen me in the gray uniform, and I knew that it would humble me in their presence. The feeling of being an impersonal commodity overwhelmed me, and my innocence cried from within for help. None was to be found within these walls.

I had to return to Texas, to face my accusers and show them their charges were wrong. The people of my native city could have no influence on the mechanics of the court. What I was about to face was real, not some movie script. My thoughts trailed into the noise of the approaching guard's steps. The remaining prisoners returned to their individual cells, and the sequence of bar doors closing and opening was commenced.

I almost wanted to stay in my cell rather than face the indifferent person in whose hands my immediate future depended. Would I have to remain in jail until Texas police came to get me? I was about to find out.

The guard led me to the elevator and then on to a large holding cell on the first floor. I was soon joined by two other men in the holding tank across the hall from the processing counter. Their faces were drawn and unshaven. Their eyes, deep and circled with darkness, seemed to trace the walls and bars, perhaps seeking a way out. I could only assume mine were as theirs.

Sheriff Smith walked silently to the main desk to read over the docket for the day's court session. I chuckled to myself, wondering how he would react to my name on the list. I soon found out, as he turned and approached my cage.

"Well, well! You never know who you'll see in here," he said, grinning, pleased with his moment of humor.

"How are you, Sheriff?" I laughed, in response to the situation.

"Just fine. And you?"

"I'm kind of tied up at the moment, but otherwise not too bad," I replied, grinning.

"How do you like the new jail?" he asked, not really trying to be sarcastic. He had been trying to upgrade the city's "correctional facilities" for many years, and he was proud of the fruits of his labor.

"It's a nice place to visit, but I wouldn't want to stay," I replied, chuckling. "It hasn't been too bad. Everyone has treated me fairly. I know they are just doing their jobs."

The sheriff smiled with pride. He had always been a fair and honest man, as far back as I could remember. His position was all but predetermined prior to every election because of his good record and popularity. "What is this about extradition?" he asked.

"A county in Texas is accusing me of an armed robbery that I don't know anything about!" The volume of my response surprised me.

"Don't worry about it," he said with a poker face. He turned and walked away, and with him went a tremendous burden from my shoulders. I did not know what he could do for me, but I knew he would do what he was able.

The doors of the elevator opened, unleashing the sound of cooped-up men. A guard approached our door and, after opening it, walked the three of us to the main desk. A handcuff was put on one of my wrists, chained to a cuff that was placed on the wrist of a man already in the "daisy chain" of prisoners. A second cuff was put on my other wrist, and I was chained to one of the other men who had been in the holding cell with me.

We were marched in chains to the exit door. Although it was cold and raining heavily outside, the sight of nature after three days' confinement filled me with hope. I found myself doing a cancan with another member of our chained gang.

"Everyone into the vans!" hollered the guard. If it had not been raining, I presumed we would have walked to the courthouse, which was only about a hundred yards away. The mood of the others seemed as light as my own, on the surface, but beneath that was a nervousness that could be detected in all of us, crowding our senses.

The air was very cold in the garage that housed the vans. The humidity, usually a bother in such cold air, felt good in my lungs. The yellow-orange van doors were opened. We were divided into two groups, to be rejoined at the courthouse. Large doors were raised electrically after we had been locked into the prisoner carriers, and the two vehicles backed down a short driveway to the road. I tried losing myself in the motion of the windshield wiper blades, trying not to imagine the courtroom, but the sight of the van in front of us brought me back to reality. The trip was too short.

Getting out of the van was difficult, because my wrists were being pulled to their respective sides of my body, making balance difficult. The rain felt good on my skin, despite being very cold. The two lines of men were again made one in the hallway inside. There were offices on either side of us, with dutiful bureaucrats working hard, here of their own free will.

A guard told us to move to the open door on the right, at the end of the hall, and to do so silently. The plastic sandals shuffled almost in unison down the boring hall, fearfully carrying us to unknown futures. One at a time, men ahead of me turned to the right and disappeared from the hall.

The door led into two dull yellow rooms, walls covered with graffiti and stained by cigarette smoke. The smaller room was much like the holding cell in the jailhouse, with a front wall and door of bars. The second room was larger, its walls lined by wooden benches that jutted from the walls. The door was a framework of pipe, fitted with hurricane fencing. The smaller room was the same dull yellow. The room's paint was chipped and marred by thousands of burns from cigarettes nervously smoked by others waiting. Stale, smoke-scented air filled my lungs, and I resigned myself to being captive of a system I had grown up believing was justified. From within these rooms it looked anything but that.

It did not take long for the room to become cloudy with smoke. Many of the men around me smoked butts they found on the benches or the floor. The temperature was steadily increasing. We were doing all that we could do: nothing. Despite attempts by several of my roommates, one could not pace a hole in the floor or lean one through the walls. Some bondsman was walking around the room, asking, "Are you Carl Johnson?" He had what looked like a scorecard in his hand, with several names checked off his list. He stood a chance of losing bond money. Part of me hoped Carl would not show up.

Eventually, I joined the others trying to pace a hole in the floor, thinking about my case. *Why couldn't the police give me a definite date for the crime? Where the hell is Weimar?* I could not discern answers for the thousandth time, or so it seemed. *What are my parents thinking, sitting in the courtroom? Is Karen there?* My feet and head were aching.

I began looking around for someone with a cigarette, as I'd finished my last one, and noticed a nearby fellow pulling one from his pack. I approached him.

"Can I bum a smoke?" I asked.

"Yeah, sure thing," he said, reaching into his pocket. He looked back at me. "Hey! I know you from somewhere, don't I?"

I looked at his face discerningly, trying to place its familiarity. He remembered before me.

"You went to Kempsville High School, didn't you?" he asked.

"Yeah. I graduated in '75."

"You're Mike Crabtree, aren't you?" he piped.

"Yeah, that's me," I replied.

"Man, I didn't recognize you with the short hair and the mustache. How have you been doing?"

"All right, I guess. I've been working on an oil rig out in Texas," I said.

"That's good money, isn't it?" he asked.

"Yes, it is, pretty good."

"Do you remember who I am?"

"I remember your last name: Jacobs. But I can't remember your first name."

"It's Alan. Alan Jacobs," he replied.

It had been more than three years since I had seen him. I never really got to know him, but knew who he was. He was always finding a new way to get into trouble, although most of them were harmless pranks.

"What in the world are you in for, Mike?" he asked.

"I'm wanted on a fugitive warrant from Texas. They say I was in on an armed robbery, but I don't know anything about it," I explained.

"Man, you couldn't have done anything like that. It's not you."

"Just try telling that to a cop when you are in handcuffs," I sarcastically replied. "This is my extradition hearing. I'm waving extradition, to go back and find out the whole story."

"Man, that's a bummer. I hope you get it straightened out," he said, genuinely.

The Sergeant at Arms stepped inside the front room from the courtroom, a stern look on his face. "Court is in session," he stated. "Cut the noise down." He stepped into the back room where Alan and I were seated, looked around, and then proceeded back to the courtroom.

I looked back at Alan. "What are you in for?" I quietly asked him.

He grinned. "Drunk in public, disorderly conduct, and pissing in public," he answered.

"How did that happen?"

"I was on my way home from a keg party and there was no place to take a leak, so I had my friend pull off on a dark road and I got out. A pair of headlights came up from behind me and stopped. The next thing I know, a spotlight was shined on me from the car, and a voice shouts out not to move." He paused. "They caught me red-handed." We both laughed.

People were being called to court. The conversation had been a nice diversion, but my nerves told me to get up. I wished Alan luck, thanked him for the smoke, and returned to my previous spot near the far end of the bench. Six or seven more men were called to court, including Alan. The door opened and a man with a somber face trudged in, accompanied by a guard. "Michael Crabtree! Michael Crabtree is next," boomed the guard.

I stood, my blood falling to my toes, leading me to feel somewhat faint. Approaching the door to the courtroom, I heard: "The Commonwealth of Virginia versus Michael Wayne Crabtree," from the Sergeant at Arms on the other side of the open door.

A chill hit me as I marched from the hot, smoky cells into the courtroom. I glanced around, spotting my parents, Karen, and my friend and former roommate, Terry.

The judge's bench, rising from the floor to my right, was made of finely finished wood. Sheriff Smith was standing just in front of the handrail separating the action from the gallery. I wanted to crawl into some hole in the woodwork. The guard stopped me in front of the bench and turned me to face the judge. The judge appeared to be of Italian descent, tall and slender, with black hair except for silver streaks along his temples. I supposed he was probably in his early- to mid-forties.

The hearing was brief. The prosecuting attorney, a red-haired man with small spectacles, began. "Your Honor, the defendant has agreed to waive extradition. The Commonwealth would like the Texas officials notified as expediently as possible."

"Does the defense have any statements?" the judge asked coldly.

"If it pleases the court," the public defender replied," the defendant has waived extradition in the hopes of clearing himself of the charges more quickly. He has been an upstanding member of this community for many years, and he has many people in this area who would come forward as character references ..."

"The court is not interested in his past," interrupted the judge. I felt shot down before the battle was begun. "Mr. Crabtree has been living in Texas," he continued, "and the court cannot be sure of his activities there." He paused, looking down at me.

"Because Mr. Crabtree has not been previously arrested on any charges," the public defender replied, "the defense believes it is justified in asking for a conditional release, until the Texas officers come for him."

"Does the Commonwealth have any comments?" the judge asked, looking at the red-haired fellow.

"The People believe that the request is justified, although they believe a bond should be set according to the gravity of the allegation against the defendant," he said.

"The Court agrees with the Commonwealth on that point," the judge stated. "Armed robbery is a serious offense, and a bond of ten thousand dollars is not unreasonable. Is that in agreement with the parties involved?"

"The Commonwealth will agree to that."

"The defense will agree also," said the public defender.

It was finally decided. I could leave jail ... for now. The judge looked at me. "Is your father in the courtroom?" he asked.

"Yes, sir, he is," I replied, raising my handcuffed hands to point him out in the gallery. The judge called for my father. He stood.

"Mr. Crabtree," the judge began, "you can sign what is known as a property bond on any property you own in this state. It is, in essence, a lien against your property. Should your son violate the conditions of the bond, you would forfeit the lien against your property. Do you understand what I have told you?"

"Yes, I do, Your Honor," my father replied.

"Do you wish to sign a property bond for his release?"

My father looked at me, his demeanor unquestioning while looking into my eyes, and then back at the judge. "Yes, I do."

The judge signaled to an attendant, who took my father from the courtroom to assist him with the bond forms. The judge then turned to me, sternly stating, "Michael, your father is risking his property for your benefit. The Court does not know of your innocence or guilt concerning the crime in Texas. It is, because of your absence of past trouble, trusting you to fulfill the bond agreement. Do you understand?"

"Yes, I do," I weakly replied, slightly trembling.

"Let the records show," the judge stated, "that the defendant has been released on a property bond, to willingly turn himself in to the Texas officials. Saturday, the sixth of January, should give you sufficient time to get there," he added, looking at me. I nodded in agreement. "The defendant will meet with the Texas officers of

Colorado Country by five o'clock PM Texas time on the sixth of January." He pounded his gavel. "Court is adjourned." Saying this, he stood, towering above all others in the room.

"Thank you, Your Honor!" I said.

The judge turned and left through a door behind the bench. The Sergeant at Arms led me back to the cell to join the others.

My feet were striding on air, and a song was dancing in my head. I was getting out! I could not believe it. The four days seemed like years. I thanked God for my parents. We prisoners were joined again, in chains, and marched to the vans. I was last. The trip back to the jail was quiet, except for Alan Jacobs congratulating me on getting out.

Upon arriving at the jail, we were walked to the holding cell. "The last one is to be released," one guard told the other, who was watching our progress toward the cell.

"Don't put him into the cell," said an officer behind the processing desk. His statement was unexpected. I anticipated several hours of bureaucratic red tape before being released. "Mr. Crabtree," he continued, with a noticeably respectful change in tone, "please go over to the laundry room, exchange your uniform for your clothes, and then return to this desk."

As the desk officer finished speaking, Sheriff Smith rang the bell at the front door to the holding area. "Just a minute," the desk officer said. He electrically unlocked the door.

The sheriff walked in and stopped at the bar door between the desk area and the front door, looking at me with a big smile. The desk officer unlocked the bar door with the push of a button, after first locking the outer door.

"I told you to relax," the sheriff said as he approached me. "What are you doing?"

"I was about to get my clothes back," I replied.

"Well, follow me." He walked me to the laundry room. "Mr. Crabtree would like his clothes," the sheriff told a man working in the room. The man hurriedly retrieved my clothes, bringing with them a listing of things I had checked in.

"There should be a pair of jeans and T-shirt in this bag," he said, handing me a small cloth bag, "plus some things someone brought for you."

The bag contained my shirt and pants, a few changes of underwear and socks, and a pair of tennis shoes. My parents told me the previous day that they had brought the bag, but I had not received it.

I changed clothes in a nearby restroom, the prison garb lying in a pile on the floor. I folded the coveralls and left the restroom, returning to the laundry room, where Sheriff Smith was still waiting. I placed the uniform and sandals on the counter.

"Is this everything that you left?" the sheriff asked.

"Yes, sir," I replied, signing the form the laundry worker had handed to me.

"Let's go this way," the sheriff said, striding away from me, down a hall through which I had not passed in my stay. We walked at a brisk pace. The sheriff, a very busy man, probably did not realize how rapidly he walked. It took little time for us to reach another counter. A man in a gray tweed suit, his hairline creeping like horns above his temples, stood up and walked from behind his paperwork-covered desk. The dark mustache gave him a very continental look.

"Hello, sheriff," the man said in a mild voice. "How are you today?"

"Fine, thank you," the sheriff replied. "Do you have the property bond for Mr. Crabtree?" he asked, gesturing in my direction.

"Oh, yeah," the man replied, "that's the one you had hurried through, isn't it?"

"Is the paperwork finished?" the sheriff asked, not acknowledging the man's question.

"Yes, sir," he replied, picking up a nearby document set. "Mr. Crabtree, just sign here," he pointed at a line on the first page, "and here" pointing to the second page, "and here" pointing to a third page.

I signed as quickly as possible, the entire morning's events now becoming plain to me. The sheriff had arranged it all, now hurrying the final release process. I felt honored. A smile radiated from my face as we returned to the main processing desk. The guard returned my wallet, shoes that my parents had left, and coat. He also gave me a check from the city for twenty dollars that my father had deposited into an account for me to use at the prison canteen.

"Well, I guess that is it," said the sheriff, extending his hand. "Is everything there?"

"Yes, sir," I responded. "I can't thank you enough, Sheriff," I said with honest humility. I vigorously shook his hand.

He reached into his suit pocket and gave me a card. It had the city's Sheriff Department seal, his name and title, address, and telephone numbers. "If you can use my help in Texas," he said, "legally or as a character reference, I'll do whatever I can for you."

I reached toward him to again shake his hand. "Thank you, sir," I humbly replied.

With that, I turned, put on my coat, and went first through the door of bars completing the cement-walled cage and then through the outer door with its brick façade. There, in the rain, a white car was waiting for me. Cold, wet, dreary skies did not matter, as two relieved parents reunited with a much-relieved son.

Twenty-fifth Anniversary Reception: Fitting In

"Hi, Hon," Mom said as I opened the white Ambassador's back door. "How does it feel to be out?"

"It feels great!" I replied as I sat.

"The others are looking forward to seeing you," Mom continued.

"Believe me, I can't wait to see them," I said with relief.

"We're glad you can be at the reception," she added.

The long, straight road from the courthouse complex to the Kempsville area, which natives referred to as "the Five Mile Stretch," seemed every inch of its name. My nerves were still on edge, but it was an excited peak, not a dull, painful blade. There was so much to be done, so much to be thought out. I had tried in vain to keep the reception out of my mind when in jail. I did not know if I would be out in time, and I doubted I would. If not for Sheriff Smith, I would most likely have remained behind bars until the Texas police came for me.

As we turned down Hatteras Road, where my family lived, it had never looked better, despite the rain. My older sister, Cindy, and her fiancé were there. My youngest brother, Bobby, had gone somewhere in his Blazer. Dad's Buick was also gone, so I supposed that Joyce was also out somewhere. It appeared I would have time to relax before the final preparations for the reception.

We pulled into the driveway, behind the dark blue Chrysler Newport Custom that I had left behind when I hitchhiked to Texas. A heavy freeze had caused the engine's freeze plug to pop out, and the engine was not ready to go when I was, almost a year earlier. I slapped it on the fender as I passed, to say hello, as we walked to the door. I laid my coat on the dining room table and strode into the kitchen. There was nothing out of the ordinary at home.

My mother told me my brother, Paul, was out with a friend; sister, Barbara, was at track practice; Cindy and her fiancé, Pat, were watching television; and Joyce and Bobby were at the church, preparing things for the reception. The house was practically empty: that was not out of the ordinary; we had always been a busy family.

I sat down at the kitchen table. Mom had put on a pot of coffee and set an ashtray on the table, amid the numerous articles lying about the table surface. This same table had been the site of many very lengthy, deep discussions about our differing perceptions of life. She was from a small town in Ohio and I from the growing suburbs of a large metropolitan area. She had always been one to trust what she was told. I trusted what I was shown.

Mom's father was an honest and hardworking construction contractor. He believed in the value of hard work, integrity, and fair dealings with all persons. He was staunchly Catholic, his third-generation Irish piety and devotion as strong as his will and his powerful, rough hands. Grandpa Snyder could be unflinching in his criticism of personal irresponsibility, convinced that all actions fit into black and white categories.

Yet beneath his rough and calloused exterior was a huge and compassionate heart. Grandpa Snyder was sentimental and sympathetic. He was generous to a fault. When his construction crews had no work. he continued paying them, depriving his own family in order to ensure that the workers remained whole. He commanded respect and rightly deserved it.

Mom's unquestioning Catholic faith came from her father, as did her honesty, will, sense of integrity, and compassion. In our community, she was well respected. She was generous in giving of her time to volunteer activities.

She had started an organization called "Block Mothers" many years previously. Block Mothers was a group of volunteers whose homes were open to children in cases of emergency. It was formed primarily as a means to combat child molestation. If a child was in a neighborhood other than his or hers and got injured or was approached by a possible molester, the child could knock on a Block Mother's door and trust that the person who answered would help.

I had always been proud of her for her volunteer work. When we were children, the schools taught us about the Block Mother program and informed us that we would be safe at a Block Mother home. Mom made presentations to schoolchildren throughout the city, explaining the program and making certain the children knew how to identify the Block Mother signs. If we were in trouble in a strange neighborhood, we were to look for the Block Mother sign in windows of homes.

As a result of her work, Mom was known and respected by the city's civic leaders. The mayor was a good friend. My mother was not outwardly affected by it, seeming to take it with a dismissing nonchalance. It led to a high level of personal accomplishment expectation in me. She believed that contributing to one's community was a duty. As a result, her actions formed the community around her. Perhaps the same type of organization as Block Mothers would have formed had she not done it, but that was a hypothetical consideration because she *did* form it. She had made something occur in her community, perceiving the need.

Block Mothers soon became organized in other cities across Virginia and the nation. Mom sat on panels with representatives from local police and even the FBI. It never went to her head. What she did, she did for her community from a sense of personal obligation. That sense of obligation had been imbedded in my expectations for myself.

Mom was witty and loved to laugh. In that regard, she took after her mother. Mom loved music and loved to dance. As a girl, she had taken tap dancing. As children, we spent hours with her, learning how to sing in harmony and how to dance.

Whenever Grandma Snyder, my mother's mother, came, she would play the piano for us and have us sing with her. Sometimes she would play this one song, and we children would walk around the quadrangle formed by the dining room, kitchen, living room, and den halls, walking around the open halls as long as Grandma played her song at a slow pace. When Grandma sped up her playing, we would speed up our pace. She would play faster and faster—and we would go faster and faster—until we were nearly running, laughing the whole time.

We would be exhausted by the time she had finished playing. Of course Grandma Snyder almost always did this just before it was time for us to brush our teeth and get ready for bed. I didn't figure that out until I was no longer a kid. Prior to that, it was simply having fun with Grandma.

As long back as I could remember, during her days while doing housework, Mom always had a tune on her lips—whether singing, humming, or whistling. She was quite a whistler.

These days, she would go with some friends to retirement homes, entertaining the residents with songs dating back fifty years. She had a good singing voice. She knew all these songs by heart. Persons attending her sing-alongs would request songs by title, by humming a tune or providing some of the lyrics. She amazed them with her memory of all these old songs. When the television show "Name That Tune" came on, we children begged her to go on it, to show what she could do. She amazed us as much as her sing-along audiences.

You could always tell when Mom had gone to a retirement home and had been informed that one of her audience had died since her last visit. She would come home saddened by the loss of a friend. She became friends with these older people. She brought forth their laughter, their memories of younger, vibrant bodies, times, passions, and dreams, stemming from associations with music that influenced or were memorably part of their lives.

In many cases, her visits were the only regular ones many of these old people received, their own families having placed them into someone else's care: out of sight, out of mind. You could see the hurt on her face, that people were put away to die alone, but she went every week to different retirement homes, spreading her emotions, compassion, and love.

When Mom told us her decision about a behavior or a requested course of action, there was no debating it with her: At least not when she gave her instruction. We could talk with her about her decision at a later time, but she would not be questioned when they were made. Such talks had become discussions, over time, especially since I had gone to college. The "social norms," especially sexual activity among unmarried persons, had been changing. She believed the changes to be for the worse, as the permissiveness was against her religious faith. She had her other reasons too, having to do with human emotions and mutual responsibilities.

As I matured she allowed me to raise subjects, such as premarital sex, that had previously been closed to discussion. Many of her answers remained: "That is what I believe, and you can have your own beliefs." Our discussions would frequently reach such impasses, but there was no animosity in the idea exchanges. We had reached such an impasse in this discussion, so I changed the subject.

"I'd like to cover what we do and do not know about the case," I began.

"We still haven't found out anything more from Texas," Mom replied.

"I don't know what their problem is," I heatedly stated, "but if they are putting me through this without any real evidence of my involvement, then I'm going to sue the hell out of them!"

"I'm sure there is something that would imply your participation," Mom said.

"There'd better be," I sharply replied, "because I'm sick of this not knowing."

My father walked into the kitchen from the television room. He leaned against the refrigerator, awaiting an entrance into our conversation. My mother looked over her shoulder at his approach and then looked once again at me.

"We have the number of that attorney in Houston," Mom said. "It's over on the counter. You really need to contact him this afternoon."

"Have you talked to him yet?" I asked.

"Yes," Dad replied, "I have."

"Well, I'll talk to him later," I responded. "Do the Burnetts know about all of this?"

"Yes," Mom answered. "David saw the patrol cars in the court. He thought there might be trouble there until he saw you being led to the car. They called Saturday night, and I told them what had gone on. I'm sure they'd want to see you."

"I'll go when I get back from the store. I need to get some cigarettes," I replied. "Dad, can I use the car?"

He didn't say anything, just threw the car keys to me, turned, and went back into the television room. His eyes were bloodshot and surrounded by dark circles, contrasting the growing number of gray hairs on his otherwise dark head of hair. I watched him walk away, wondering how all this had affected him. Outwardly, it did not seem to change him much, but I knew it had, from the frustration apparent on his face. He had always seemed in command; I was not used to seeing him this way.

"Your dad has really taken this hard," Mom said, noticing that I was thinking about my father.

"I can imagine," I replied.

"No, you *can't*," she said emphatically, her voice taut. "He has laid awake the last few nights. He cried last night, telling me he wished he could have shown you kids how he felt as you grew up. Your father is not a man of words. He was always at all of your ballgames, and your school functions, always supporting you."

She paused, tears coming to her eyes. "Do you know," she began, her voice cracking from emotion, "that last night was the first time in a long time that he told me that he *loves* me?" She wiped her eyes. "He still can't tell me why, but I *know* he loves me." Tears continued building in her eyes as she stopped.

The quiet made me uncomfortable, not knowing what to do or say in response. Eventually I stood, putting the keys into my pocket. "Do you need anything from the store?" I quietly asked. She gave me a short verbal list and twenty dollars, and I headed out to the car.

Handling a car felt odd, as my body was sluggish and stiff from four days of limited use. The bars were good for doing pull-ups and the bunk for sit-ups, but I only tried them once, with the small guy in the next cell. We were not quick to revert to exercise to avoid boredom, as sleep was the preferred escape.

Mom was right, I reflected during my drive to the store and back. Dad had been our coach in youth athletics. He had taught us how to catch, throw, how to hit a baseball. He'd taught us to mean what we said and to not say anything we did not mean. He helped us with homework, but more in explaining the basic concepts to be learned. He was always proud of us and attended all of our athletic and school functions.

Dad was an extremely intelligent and respected engineer. He had already received citations from two different US presidents for his exemplary work as a civil servant working with the Navy. Dad had traveled frequently in his work, when we were younger children. For that reason, he had always put my mother in immediate charge of the house's affairs and his children's upbringing. Dad only became involved in disciplining us as a last resort, and usually only after Mom had informed us that she was "going to tell your father." Of course, that threat alone was most often sufficient to change our behavior. Dad was not at all violent. It was just that we had enormous respect for him and did not want to disappoint him.

Two years previously, during the summer after I returned from my first year at college, one morning Dad and I were walking back to his garden in the backyard. His garden was his hobby, and he produced delicious tomatoes, peppers, cucumbers, squash, beans, and okra. Dad had been raised in Greensboro, North Carolina. When he was older, his parents, he, and his sister moved to Chapel Hill, where his parents still had a twenty-acre parcel of land atop a hill.

His mother was a great cook in the Southern tradition of vegetables. What she could do with green beans and corn, or the wild blackberries we would pick in the field behind their Chapel Hill, North Carolina, home! Who cared if we got chigger bites all over our tiny legs as children? A taste of her blackberry cobbler was worth a few itchy bites any day.

"Dad?" I asked this morning as we walked. "You have never really told me much about yourself." I walked a few paces behind him, as he carried his pail and a small paring knife to collect okra.

He stopped walking, turned, and looked at me with a slightly puzzled look on his face. He sort of shrugged. "It seemed to me," he began, "that there wasn't that much to tell." He turned and resumed his walk toward the garden.

"It's just that," I replied. "How can I know who I am if I don't know who you are?"

He kept walking. "I'll tell you anything you want to know."

"But, Dad," I said, "I don't even know what to ask about you."

He paused, pondering. "I don't remember much about my young years," he said. "I had a newspaper route when I was a boy. I'd get up at four o'clock every morning, ride my bike to the newspaper drop place, and fold the newspapers for my route. That was every day, rain or shine. After delivering them, I'd go home and get ready for school." By now, he had reached the first row of okra plants. He set down his pail, bent over, and pushed the plant's leaves aside, seeking pods of the right size.

"How many years did you do that?" I asked.

"Oh, I guess four or five," he answered.

"What else do you most remember?"

He dropped a few okra pods in the pail and then stood. He was starting to perspire, as the morning was very humid and warm. He stated, "I remember that my father worked in the textile mills, in Greensboro. He worked many, many hard hours." He wiped some sweat from his forehead. "And, I remember, one day, I told myself I wasn't going to work in the mills."

He looked at me. "Your grandfather didn't have much of an education. He taught himself enough math to keep up with the records for textile output." He bent back over and began checking another plant for pods. "He had this notebook, in which he kept his calculations for the mill. I came across it one day and was fascinated. He had all of these longhand calculations written in it."

He glanced up at me. "I told myself I needed to learn numbers. If I could learn numbers, I could do something with it." He cut a few pods, dropping them into the pail followed by a hollow thunk. "There was this one teacher who liked me. She saw that I liked numbers, and she helped me learn. I was good at it."

He stood and grinned. "I remember when I was a senior in high school. The high school math teacher was sick. My old math teacher asked if I would teach as a substitute."

"That's neat," I told him.

"I got a paycheck from the county for being a substitute teacher." He nodded as though the past memory had long ago been placed in the insignificance category. Now, it was not insignificant. It was part of him, one of the decisions that he had made, resulting in a beneficial outcome. "I was proud of that," he said. "So was your grandpa."

Both Mom and Dad had been good students. They never told us we had to succeed or excel, only that we had to do our best. If we did our best, no one could expect more of us. There was only one catch: only we would know if we had done our best. It was the last question to be answered each night before going to bed: had you done your best?

My approach to the corner at which I was to turn right into our neighborhood required my driving attention, and I returned to present tasks from amidst the memories of my conversation with Dad. The house that I approached was not just a residence. It had become the cornerstone from which the future of each child had been built. It had been filled with love, discipline, respect, and expectation of personal integrity. Its walls were filled with memories of happy times with friends, music and dance, laughter, and good—if simple—food.

Upon my return from the store, I opened the refrigerator, got a beer, and left the house to walk to the Burnetts', just down the street. The Burnetts had been our neighbors for fifteen years. We had shared Christmases, Halloweens, and birthdays. My family had six children and theirs four, and we had grown up together as close friends. They were fine people.

I walked slowly through the light drizzle, in no hurry to reach their house. Our street was an appreciated sight, bringing fond memories of street ballgames, footraces and bicycle races, and the general happy adventures we had as children.

"Well, hello!" Sharon said in surprise as she opened the front door. "Come on in!"

Sharon, now nineteen, a little more than two years younger than me, had grown to become an attractive young woman. Even as a young girl she had been pretty, with very long, beautiful blonde hair. The stick figure of her youth had filled out well, and I found myself watching her walk as I followed her into the kitchen.

"Look who's here!" Sharon announced as she entered the kitchen ahead of me.

"Hello, there, Mike," Mr. Burnett said as he extended a hand. "When did you get out?"

"Around noon," I replied. "I was released on a property bond."

Mrs. Burnett had stepped away from her work at the countertop and stood behind her husband's chair.

"Hey, Barry!" Mr. Burnett hollered, to his oldest son. "Come in the kitchen and see who's here!"

I heard Barry walk from within the room that they had added to the back of their two-story home. Barry, a year younger than me, and I had been close friends since they moved into this home. As friends, we had done a lot together. We had had our fights as well as our good times, just as any two close friends do. He and I had drifted apart since I began college, but there was still that bond shared by two persons who have helped each other grow up.

"Oh my gosh!" he exclaimed, startled. "How are ya?" He shook my hand vigorously. Barry was a little taller than me, slightly heavier, and had sandy brown hair that swept across his forehead from the part on one side.

"I'm okay, I guess. The last four days have drained me. Now I have to get ready for the reception."

"Tell me, Mike," Barry paused, raising a hand to his chin. "What's the story here?"

I spent the next ten minutes trying to explain everything I knew and did not know about the case. Some of the story came out vehemently, especially details about my stay in jail. The beer wet my lips and lubricated my speech, and the Burnetts were amazed by the events of the past days. David and Mike, the two other Burnett children, had appeared from elsewhere in the house, so the whole family was listening.

"I don't see how they could think you had done that," Barry said at my monologue's conclusion, scratching his head.

"Well they do," I replied. "I have to turn myself in to the Colorado County police by Saturday."

"This whole thing is *crazy*!" Sharon added.

"Yeah, but it's *real*, unfortunately," I said. I got up from the chair I had been sitting in since beginning my explanation. "Well, I have to get moving. I've got to go help out at the church."

Mr. Burnett rose with my words. "Mike, it's good to have you back. This thing really worried us," he said, extending his hand, which I shook.

"It's got me worried, too," I told him. "Hopefully it will all be cleared up soon." I turned to retrace my steps out. Barry joined me, opening the door ahead of me.

"Mike, I still can't believe it," he stated, shaking his head. "You'll be back around to see us before you go back to Texas, won't you?"

"Oh, yeah. I plan on it. I'll probably be leaving Thursday evening. I'll be seeing you tonight, won't I?"

"We'll be there," he said. "Wouldn't miss it."

"Great! I'll see you tonight, then," I replied, shaking his hand.

Walking down the steps away from the door, as Barry closed it behind me, I noticed my brother's Blazer and my father's Buick at the house. Joyce and Bobby must have finished working at the church.

It was no longer drizzling, the sky having showered slowly and steadily all midday. The street was quiet, abandoned because of the rain. Normally it would have had children playing somewhere nearby.

"Well, hello bro'!" Bobby said as I came through the dining room toward the kitchen. We shook hands and I went to the refrigerator to get another beer. "It's good to have you back!"

"It's good to be back." I sat again at the kitchen table.

"Everything's finished at the church," he said.

I heard footsteps coming down the stairs. Joyce rounded the corner into the dining room, coming toward the kitchen. Her eyes lit up as she saw me and a large smile came to her face. "Hi, Mike! Welcome back!"

I stood up and we embraced, squeezing tightly for a moment. Her big brother was back, even if just for a few days. As I looked at her I felt I had let her down. When this would end, I did not know, but I could not fail in clearing my name. If I did, there was no telling how she and Barbara would think of me. Their opinions were important to me; I did not want to feel that I had let them down.

"You ought to see the church," Joyce said. "It's really pretty."

"When did you finish working on it?" I asked.

"About a half hour ago," she answered.

I took a swallow of beer and rested the bottle on the table. "When is Barbara due back?"

"She should be back around two-thirty," Bobby replied. It was already two o'clock. Six hours remained before the party.

"You'd *better* get hold of Mr. Paris," my mother interjected as she entered the kitchen from the television room, pointing a finger at me.

"Okay, I will," I replied in a surrendering tone. I was putting it off. For the moment, I did not want to think about the case, putting it into the back of my mind as if, back there, it could not harm me.

Sooner or later, I would have to deal with it. Right now, it was to be later.

"You should go see the Tachés," Mom said while fixing a sandwich for my father. "I told Irene about your arrest, yesterday at Mass. She cried. I know they'll want to see you before you go."

"Are they going to be there tonight?"

"No," Mom replied. "Irene said she wasn't feeling well, and that she would have to stay inside today."

"I guess I'll go over tomorrow. I'll be going over to see the Jernigans too."

Mom looked at me with one of her you're-not-doing-what-I'm-telling-you looks. "Please call Mr. Paris."

"Mom," I stated, as in self-defense, "right now I just want to relax. The last thing I want to do at the moment is to think about going to Texas."

"I can understand that," she said, hesitating, her tone a lead-in to a "but" statement following close behind, "but it's got to be done."

"All right. Yes, ma'am," I said, surrendering. "Where is the number?"

"Right here," she replied, handing me the piece of paper beside her.

I walked to the kitchen counter and dialed the number using the telephone beside the stove. A soft voice with a slight drawl answered the ringing. "Good afternoon. Evans and Paris."

"Hello. My name is Michael Crabtree. I'd like to speak with Mr. Paris, if I could."

"He's out to lunch. Could you call him about three o'clock? He should be back by then."

"Okay, I will."

"I'll tell him you called," she stated, the drawl now more apparent in the word "called." She was definitely Texan.

"Thank you," I replied. "Goodbye." I was almost glad he was out.

My back was to the crowd now gathered in the church's huge foyer. "Hello, Karen?" I asked, huddled among the coats next to the telephone. "How are you?"

"I'm *fine*," she said, her annoyance apparent. "Where are you?"

"I'm at the church. We're having my parents' twenty-fifth wedding anniversary reception here."

"That's real nice," she sarcastically replied.

Neither of us spoke for several seconds, and the silence was tense. I could only imagine her anger at me for not calling since my release earlier that afternoon. Fishing for something to acknowledge her presence in court, I stammered for a moment before speaking.

"I, uh ... wanted to thank you for being in court today," I finally uttered.

"Oh, *really*?" she snapped back. "You sure wouldn't have known it. You didn't even nod or signal in any way. As far as I could tell, you looked only once in that direction."

"Karen!" I replied, this time anger building within me. "The situation was not one in which I could have waved at you." I did not pause before continuing: "I was humiliated, and all you can think about was the fact that I didn't signal to you in some way! Standing up there in that gray outfit was *hell*."

I felt like hanging up. Karen seemed to have no sympathy for what I had been through. She was not unfeeling, but I had kept her hanging on for so long that she had a right to question opening herself to me. My feelings about her still puzzled me. On the one hand, I felt like hanging up, telling her to forget it all, but on the other, I wanted her by me. I began questioning my motives for continuing to see her. Neither of us had anything to say for a moment.

"I'm sorry," she said meekly. "That was selfish of me."

There was no reply on my part. I was still not ready to speak. Minutes seemed to pass, no words spoken.

"I was going to see you when the reception is over, if that is okay with you," I finally said.

"It's okay. I'll be here all evening. I'm not doing anything," she replied with exaggerated boredom. She paused. "I wish I could be there with you."

"Well ... after all that has gone on recently," I began, "I wanted to spend the evening with my parents. The reception is sort of a gift to them from us children. I hope you understand."

"I understand," she stated. "I also understand that if I'm going to be part of your family, I'll need to get closer to your parents and relatives."

"Karen, I know ..." I responded, hesitating. "Give it time, please." I was silent for a moment. "I'll call you when the reception is breaking up."

"All right," she replied.

"I'll talk to you later," I said as a prelude to "goodbye."

"Michael, I love you," she said, her voice assured.

I could not respond. I was not sure, and did not want to lie to her.

"You did not reply," she stated. "What is it?"

"I'm just not sure."

"Yes, you are," she emphatically responded. "You *have* to be."

The telephone felt awkward in my hand, becoming heavy. "I'll talk to you later," I replied, my voice tense.

"Okay," she said dejectedly.

"Goodbye."

"Goodbye," she softly replied.

I hung up slowly and turned toward the activities around me. My sister, Joyce, was carrying a punchbowl from the kitchen to a serving table in the foyer of the church.

"Let me get that," I told her, quickly walking toward her.

Joyce and I had become close in recent years. For some reason we had chosen to confide in each other, especially since I began college. It began when she wrote to me about boy problems she was having in high school, and it was continuing to blossom. We now conversed about practically everything. We had differing opinions and perspectives of many subjects, which often acted as buffers for each other. My imprisonment must have been difficult for her to take, but she had not shown it. She was too busy, now, to worry about anything.

This reception had been the culmination of months of planning. There was too much work put into it to halt it because of my problems. It would have hurt me tremendously if they had decided not to have it.

It was very brisk outside, more guests bundling up as they got out of their cars and approached the church's front doors. As I passed the huge window-faced spire, carrying the punchbowl, my mind associated these guests hustling to the church in the cold and my approach to my parents' car at the jail, that afternoon. The white Ambassador's exhaust had been a plume of mist in the parking lot, with the heads of two persons looking from within for my release from jail.

Carrying the punchbowl near the front of the church, I broke my stare at the reflection on the windowpane, coming back to the present. Now helping Joyce with the punchbowl, I almost wished that Karen had been out when I called.

Our conversation had not cleared up anything. Instead, it further clouded my emotions for her with anger at her insensitivity and pushiness. She was hurrying something that I was trying to decelerate. As much as I cared for her, part of me kept withdrawing for safety. It had always withdrawn from her to safety. What would change that now?

I set the punchbowl on the table and then turned to greet more guests who had just entered the church. Taking their coats, I asked them to sign the guest register. There were old friends, new friends, church members, and those now so dear as to be considered extended family. The church foyer, with its recessed mezzanines, enveloped our party. Laughter was contagious, as my family's gatherings always led to stories, jokes, and other verbal means that persons endow with their trust of and affection for each other. Laughter, stories, and jokes existed to share emotions; otherwise, persons in their respective emotional spheres would be unable to let others glimpse inside.

Paul Peter and his wife had just walked in. I pasted a smile on my face and approached them. Mr. Peter had been my mathematics teacher in high school. He was not just a teacher to his students but a mentoring friend, and his opinion mattered very much to me.

"Hello, Mr. Peter!" I exaggeratedly exclaimed, in jest, as I shook his hand. Mr. Peter was a genuine, warm person who liked to laugh. "How the heck are you?" I asked.

"I'm doing very well, thank you," he replied, a large grin coming to his face. "And you?"

"Mrs. Peter," I stated in acknowledgment, briefly shaking her hand and taking her coat. "I could be better," I replied, turning my head to face Mr. Peter.

Mrs. Peter spotted my mother. She waved and headed in her direction.

An expression of concern spread across Mr. Peter's face. He looked into my eyes, anticipating that I wanted to say something. He knew me that well.

"I'll tell you about it later, when we are alone. How long do you expect to be here?" I asked.

"We'll be here for a while. What is the problem?" he asked with undisguised interest and concern.

I glanced around. We were alone in a room full of busy people. "This may sound odd, but I was released from jail this morning."

"*What in the world for?*" he asked in disbelief, his pitch higher and slightly louder.

"I am supposed to be a fugitive from Texas. They want me for an armed robbery that I don't know anything about," I stated matter-of-factly. I paused, to try judging his reaction.

His mouth had fallen open in astonishment. He cocked his head slightly to one side, and then looked at me as if expecting an explanation. He did not say a word, but stood, waiting for me to continue.

I unloaded my story to him, glad that he wanted it, as I had not been able to get it out of my head throughout the reception. His eyes did not lose contact with mine as he soaked in the words. Finally I finished. He still just stood there for a moment, silent.

He took a deep swallow, closed his eyes, and slowly shook his head. He glanced at the floor and then back at my face. "I don't know what to tell you," he said. "It sounds pretty rough," he added. "Good luck clearing it up."

"Thank you for listening. I've had it on my mind all evening, and had to tell someone." I reached out my hand once more. "Your opinion matters to me, and I wanted you to hear this from *me*," I said. He shook my hand. "Have a good time this evening. We are *so* glad you could make it," I honestly told him.

"I wouldn't have missed it," he replied.

"I'll see you later," I said, reaching to take his coat. I turned and walked to the coat racks, feeling better for having involved someone else in my mishap, as I was having difficulty handling it myself.

The reception went very smoothly. No one other than the Burnetts, and now Mr. Peter, had heard of my situation. To all others who inquired about my well-being, I discussed the oil industry and drilling rigs. The people of eastern Virginia had not seen a drilling rig firsthand, and the mystique of the technology and the people involved interested many of the guests.

My sister, Cindy, had given me her camera to take pictures during the reception. I weaved in and out of the small crowd that had gathered around my parents by the table where the gifts had been collected. My mother reached for the first gift, and I started taking pictures of the gifts and my parents. The remainder of the guests gathered around the table.

Seated, Mom opened the gift and began to cry tears of joy and speechless gratitude. Dad just stood there behind her, smiling as if his life depended upon it. I'd never seen him smile so broadly, for so long. Mom and Dad just glowed. No picture could capture the emotions pouring forth from them, and from the guests. It was fitting that such a celebration was taking place in a church, no matter the differences in religious belief among the guests. This was a celebration of life and lives. I began feeling tense, trying hard to fit in and forget about my situation.

Finally, the opening of gifts was over. Mom's tears, however, weren't. Joyce came over and gave my mother a hug.

Someone from the back of the gathered hollered, "Speech!" The command was echoed by others, until Mom held up a hand in acknowledgment. She looked over her shoulder at Dad. She tried drying her tears, but the parade would not be stopped.

Gaining her composure, she began to speak. "I don't know what to say ..." She paused. "Our marriage, Wayne's and mine, has been blessed with many things. Over the years many people have helped us develop, both as individuals and together. I thank God for the good friends we have. I hope the next twenty-five years are as rewarding as these have been. Thank you so much."

She broke up, surrendering to uninhibited tears. Bobby stepped forward, hugging Mom and shaking Dad's hand. As he stepped back, I placed the camera upon the table and stepped forward toward my father. I reached out and shook Dad's hand. He tightened his grip on my hand, drawing me to him. He wrapped his other arm around my shoulders and squeezed me very tightly.

My response was spontaneous, clutching to him. Tears filled my eyes. For the first time I could remember, my father was hugging me. We relaxed our grip and broke from the embrace. He was crying, as was I. I turned toward Mom, who was watching my father and me. I grabbed her in a tight hug, for a long time. Finally ending it, I turned and immediately walked to a flight of stairs and up to the church's mezzanine.

There was no longer any holding back. Anger, frustration, and fear poured from my eyes, running over my trembling hands, sobs racking me. My brother, Paul, passed by without comment.

Why had this all happened? Why had it happened now, just before the reception? When was it going to end? How was it going to end?

I dried my eyes and took several deep breaths. I walked to the mezzanine rail and peered over at the gathering, and then returned to my seat on the sofa. After several minutes, I felt composed enough to return to the party.

The Hasketts had entered. They noticed my eyes. Mr. Haskett gave me a look of understanding, and a smile. "Hello, Mike," he said.

"Hello, Mr. Haskett. Glad y'all could make it," I replied, shaking his hand. I pointed to the tables of food. "Refreshments are over there, where Mike is," I said, laughing, as their son, Mike, was stuffing his mouth with finger sandwiches.

People began meandering again, many ready to leave. I sorted through the coats, giving them back to their respective owners as they approached the door, and thanking them for coming as they exited.

Someone had turned up the music. Soon, my brothers, sisters, and some of our friends were dancing. When we were young, my mother had taught us to dance. Styles of music had changed, but we all enjoyed dancing at every opportunity. Mom taught us how to do the jitterbug and how to shag. Whoever was playing disc jockey was choosing all types of music. A song came on that Mom had used to teach me how to shag. "Come on, Mom!" I told her, taking her hand.

She and I started dancing, and the others stepped back to watch. We danced and danced until Mom was out of breath. For those minutes, my thoughts were extinguished. There was no tomorrow, no Texas, no fear—only this moment, music, and motion. The huge smile on my face was sheer enjoyment, dancing with Mom. It ended too soon.

Mom was later getting some punch when I walked up to her. "Mom," I said, "I called Karen earlier, during the reception, and told her I would make it over this evening, after we clean up."

"Why didn't you have her come to the party?" she asked, taking a sip.

"I felt this was a family thing and I didn't know if you would want her here," I replied.

"Bobby had Angie here. You could have brought Karen if you had wanted."

"I didn't know that. I'll call her now and invite her over."

The number of guests continued to dwindle. I was busy finding coats as I talked to Karen. She reluctantly agreed to come, after I assured her that her presence would make me happy. I was not certain how it would be with her there but could not find out unless she came.

As I waited for Karen, an unexpected guest arrived. Sue, my aunt by marriage, had just driven two hundred miles to get to the reception. She paraded in with her three children.

"Sue!" my mother exclaimed, making a beeline for her. She liked Sue a great amount and was glad to see her.

"Sissy, I had to be here," Sue said, calling my mother by her nickname. She had that nickname because my uncle Skip, Sue's husband and my mother's youngest brother, could not say "sister" when they were children.

"I'm glad you made it," Mom replied as they hugged.

The children entertained themselves, as youngsters are gifted at doing. Matthew and Jason, both in grade school, began exploring the church foyer and discovered the stairs to the mezzanine. Amy, a cute little toddler, was busy being cuddled by Joyce. Sue ate some sandwiches as she conversed with my mother.

Karen arrived shortly after in her green Capri. She parked by the curb in front of the foyer, under a streetlight, and fussed with her hair before getting out of the car. I watched her walk toward the church in her calf-length skirt, her hair appearing almost silver in the light as it flowed over the lapel of her coat. Karen had strong features. Her squared chin stood out from her otherwise oblong face, the long forehead of aristocracy rising from her eyes. The strength of her face was very, very beautiful.

I met her at the door, kissed her, and took her coat. The party had dwindled to relatives and the diehards, and some cleaning had begun. I escorted her through the foyer, introducing her to my relatives and the few remaining guests. Karen was always a very charming woman, intelligent and engaging, quite witty. Having returned to cleaning, leaving her talking to my parents, I occasionally glanced at her. She was so natural, flowing.

Having made her rounds and spoken to everyone, she came back over to me. "Need some help?" she asked, putting her hand lightly upon my shoulder. She had a way of raising her eyelids while subtly smiling, making her eyes sparkle and seem huge. It melted me every time.

"Sure," I replied as I folded up a table. "Thanks for the help. Why don't you see if my sisters can use some help boxing up?"

"Sure, dear," she said. She blew me a kiss and headed toward my sisters.

With Karen's help, we loaded up everything to be taken home, finished putting away the tables and sweeping the floors. She followed us to my parents' home, where we sat and talked for a while before deciding to go to her house. Karen was renting the house from her mother. Her two dogs barked from the backyard at our approach and scurried around the floor when she let them in.

We sat, quietly talking about the past. She told me of her frustration in trying to make me see how much she cared for me and about me. While in college, in Wisconsin, she had become engaged to marry a fellow she was attending school with, but she said he was a diversion, an attempt at forgetting me. It did not work, she said.

She grasped my face between her hands, kissing me gently at first, and then passionately. I put my arm behind her and leaned her back against the couch. We had no idea how long we remained there, as it did not matter.

"I've got to go to work in the morning," she said sometime much later, with a yawn, rising from the couch.

"I should be going, then," I softly replied.

"No." She paused and looked into my eyes. "I want you to stay... for a while," she continued. A look of concern came over her face. "Would that be okay?"

I did not want to lead her on, but the desire in me drove all other thoughts from my mind. "Yes, it is okay," I said.

"Are you sure?"

"Yes, I am."

She turned and walked up the steps, with me a few steps behind. Her bedroom was simple but nice. She lit some candles on her dresser, their light illuminating the room with a pale, dancing glow. I sat at the end of the bed and removed my shoes and socks, setting them by her dresser. I began to unbutton my shirt, but she stopped me. She unbuttoned it, placing it at the foot of the bed. Then she slowly took off my pants, placed them atop the shirt, and stepped back, looking at me. I removed the last piece of covering from me and got beneath the covers.

She began undressing slowly, methodically, torturing me. She turned away from me, facing the candles on her dresser. Every movement was graceful, flowing. Finally undressed, she turned.

"What do you think?" she coyly inquired, smiling.

"I think you have a beautiful body," I softly replied, stating the obvious. I stretched out my hand toward her.

She slowly approached the other side of the bed and drew back the covers. Lying beside me, she pulled the covers up to her shoulders and rested her head against my chest. She looked up, into my eyes, and gently stroked my face. Our breathing was quickening as she leaned her head back, and I kissed her tenderly. My heart was pounding in my chest.

"What do you want, Michael?" she whispered.

Preparing for the Return

Before the reception, I had called Steve Paris again at 3:00 PM. He was still not in. The secretary laughed when she realized my mistake: although three o'clock in Virginia, it was still only two o'clock in Houston.

My mother had given me a pad of paper, and I began jotting down everything pertinent to my defense. We found a large envelope and wrote "State of Texas vs. Michael W. Crabtree" across the front. I put the airline ticket for my Thanksgiving flight from Houston to Norfolk into the envelope. I made a list of the persons I had told I was returning to Virginia in December. No stone was left unturned. Paycheck stubs were included to show that I had no financial reason to rob anyone. Points of evidence were listed, as were witnesses to be contacted.

By the time we were finished, it was 4:15. I called Mr. Paris once more, from my parents' bedroom, and my father picked up the extension in the kitchen. We pelted Mr. Paris with a barrage of questions, ranging from my rights as an accused to my financial needs while I stayed in Houston. He instructed me to meet him at his office on Main Street, in Houston, at 11:00 AM on Friday the fifth. He gave me directions, the address, listed things to bring, and concluded the conversation. He was direct, professional.

I replayed the entire conversation over and over in my mind as I drove to my parents' house from Karen's. Karen had fallen asleep around 2:30 AM. I held her for some time after that. Her breathing was relaxed, her face peaceful. I stroked her hair, kissed her cheek, and got dressed. Her dogs followed me to the front door, their tails wagging nonstop.

My breath exited as a mist cloud in the early morning cold. The streetlamp next door gave ample light to walk across the yard to the white Ambassador. A slight breeze was moving through the neighborhood's quiet, the mist clouds of breath drifting away to dissipate. Stars were abundant in the sky, which was clear but for a few clouds near the moon in the sky's panorama.

No one else was on the road. Driving was a good time for thinking, and I had a lot to think about. Flight reservations to Houston had to be made, and I had not yet packed. Having no idea how long I would be in Texas, I had no idea how much clothing to pack. A suit and several sweater and pants combinations would be necessary, as well as some knock-around clothes for inside the hotel room. Mr. Paris explicitly instructed me to stay in a hotel near his office, far from the apartments where I had lived, and especially far from Kevin Silver. I was to have no contact with him during my stay.

I stopped the car at a red light. There were no other cars in sight, anywhere near the intersection. I laughed at the unnecessary delay, perceiving it as indicative of my situation.

I was not to communicate with any of my friends about the case. They were not supposed to know I was back in Texas. The money that this was going to cost began accumulating in my mind. It was going to be expensive. I just hoped it would be over quickly.

Turning onto the street to my parents' house, I saw the front porch light still on. That meant the front door was unlocked. Approaching the house, I noticed that Bobby's Blazer was not there. He must have still been at Angie's. I knew he really cared for her, but I had no idea how much. The house looked like a cross between a fortress and a used car lot. There were six cars among six drivers. Three of them were my father's. None of them were fancy, but they got us where we wanted to go. My father always said if it got you from point A to point B, and stopped in between when you needed it to, what more was it supposed to do? We children did ask that the radios work. All of them did.

Bobby arrived about 3:30 AM, walking in the front door very quietly. I was sitting on the sofa in the television room, reading my case notes and sipping a beer. Bobby grabbed a beer from the refrigerator and sat down across from me in a recliner.

"Angie is some girl," I said.

"Yeah, she is," he replied in his usual frank manner. Bobby was always direct, not embellishing or qualifying his statements.

"Do you think there will be a future for you two?" I asked.

"I don't know. I got burned by Nancy and I'm not ready to think about a future with anyone." Bobby had been engaged to Nancy. She pulled out at the last minute. Bobby took a long gulp of beer.

The conversation mingled with the sounds of the house settling and the ticking of one clock. The day had been a long, full one, and the beer nightcap relaxed us both, readying us for sleep. Bobby rose from the chair, downed his last swallow, and began walking toward the kitchen.

"Are you going to work tomorrow, Bobby?" I asked as I grabbed one edge of a sheet Mom had laid at the end of the sofa.

"Yeah. I have to be up at 6:30," he replied.

"How do you keep up with your late hours?"

He shrugged. "I just do," he said, and then stepped into the kitchen. I heard his empty bottle clink as he dropped it into the kitchen garbage. There was the sound of his steps up the stairs, and then quiet.

I stretched out the sheet and blankets, walked to the kitchen, tossed my bottle in the trash, and then got undressed and laid down to sleep. There were many people I had to see later that day; it was going to be another long one.

Everyone was partially into the day's affairs when I woke. Bobby and Joyce had gone to work. Barbara was at track practice. Cindy was getting ready to go to work. Only Paul and I were not yet up and about. My mother had fixed a pot of coffee. She and I sat down and discussed life. We spent the next four hours discussing everything from personal happiness to politics. Paul joined us for a while, probably around 11:00 AM, but he grew restless and left. The conversation inevitably returned to the case. We rehashed everything about it, as if something new and important would be gleaned, would suddenly unveil itself. Not so.

I spent the early afternoon lazily watching television before making the flight reservations. Karen was thrilled when I had called her at work, although I had told her I would before she fell asleep the previous night. We made plans for the evening.

It was around three o'clock when I drove over to the Jernigans' house. Cindy Jernigan and I had gone through school together since the eighth grade. She was a very pretty young woman, but we seemed more like siblings than available to each other. Although I took Cindy out only once on anything that resembled a date, her parents and I had become good friends, especially Mrs. Jernigan and me. She considered me one of "her boys." Surprised to see me, she greeted me at her front door with a big smile. She was silver haired, with laugh lines on her face. Cindy was the youngest of her children and was born when her next-younger sibling was almost grown.

I told Mrs. Jernigan my current situation, which astounded her. We chatted for more than an hour before her husband walked in. Mr. Jernigan was a large man, with thin white hair. He, too, was astonished by the situation, wishing me luck. We talked for a few more minutes, until I looked at my watch and informed them I had to go. My parents were expecting me home for dinner. I thanked them both for their friendship and well-wishes, telling them I would come back to see them when it was all over. They again wished me luck, and I left.

For the first time since Christmas, all of my immediate family was gathered around the dinner table. Was it solemn? My family never had solemn meals. Meals were boisterous occasions for banter and laughter. Taking after my mother, the children were sarcastic wits and wannabes, and we joked and kidded each other at any opportunity. It had long been one way we used to show our affection for each other. Our table manners were good, considering there were six children and servings were on a "whole plate of firsts eaten before seconds of anything" basis.

"Mike, you're not eating very much," my mother stated, noting my lack of appetite.

"We weren't given much food each meal in jail," I replied. Everyone became quiet for a moment. "It will take some time for me to get my stomach back to its normal quantities."

The chicken was delicious, as were the rest of the selections. Mom was a good cook, but anything would have been good compared with the bland meals behind bars. Bobby, a hardworking carpenter, voraciously cleaned up what remained in the serving bowls and platters. We picked up our empty plates, taking them to the kitchen, except for Bobby. He didn't mind, though, that we left him by himself, especially with the chicken and mashed potatoes and gravy.

"I'm going over to the Tachés'. I'll be back after that, and then Karen and I are supposed to go out," I told Mom as I rinsed my plate in the sink.

"You sure are seeing a lot of her," my mother replied as I turned and left the kitchen. "Are you two serious about each other?"

"I'm not certain yet, but it looks as if it is getting that way," I answered on my way into the living room.

The car keys were where we always put them, in a shallow bowl on a small bookshelf, between the living room and den. I was quickly out, had backed the car into the street, and was on my way. Thinking of seeing the Tachés brought a smile to my face.

They were one of the original families of our parish when the new church branched off one of the older, established parishes in the city, back in 1972. Their daughter, Connie, like Cindy Jernigan, was a schoolmate of mine during high school. Connie and I had been friends.

Over the past two years, I had sent Mr. and Mrs. Taché selections of my poems. They had been critics of sorts, not so much of style as content. Every time I would come back to Virginia, I would make it a point to stop by their house for a visit. Our discussions were contrasts of ideals which paralleled but were frequently not in unison. There was never any animosity; differing opinions were absorbed for further reflection and consideration.

Their familiar baby-blue Chrysler was in the driveway of their beautiful home. There were lights on in the den and two bedrooms on the second floor. Joy, their graying canine companion of many years, barked at the doorbell's ringing. It took a few moments for someone to get to the front door from the den, but it finally began to open.

"Hi, Mike," Marianne said in a soft but excitedly high-pitched voice. She was a slender mid-teenager, very pretty, with long, dark brown hair.

"Hello, Marianne," I replied. "Is anyone here?"

"Yeah, Mom and Dad are in the den," she answered. "Pat is at work." She always spoke very softly, sometimes requiring that close attention be paid. I had never heard her speak loudly.

"Great! I was hoping they would be here," I said.

"Come on in," Marianne said, opening the door completely, gesturing with a move of her head.

I walked through the double doors, through the large foyer, and into the kitchen, Marianne following a step or two behind me. Mrs. Taché had come into the kitchen from the den to see who was at the door.

"Mike!" she exclaimed as I entered the kitchen. "It's so good to see you."

She gave me a big hug and then stepped back, her hands upon my shoulders, to look at me. Her face, round with a very fair complexion, did not show the years of hardships and heartaches she had seen. This blithe spirit, wonderfully trusting in the teachings of Christian men of God, had continued to radiate warmth and compassion through the many trials that her life had been.

"Is it over?" she asked, peering hopefully into my face.

"No," I explained. "I have to fly back to Texas tomorrow, to turn myself in. I want to clear this up as quickly as possible."

"Did you make it to the reception last night?" she asked.

"Yes. I was released yesterday early in the afternoon."

Mrs. Taché turned back toward the den. "Warren," she loudly said. "Look who's here!"

Mr. Taché, a handsome man with dark glasses and almost-white hair, an easy-going manner and well-rounded intelligence, was a man of great sincerity and compassion—a truly good man. Mrs. Taché and I took some steps toward the den.

"Hello, Mike. Welcome back," he said, rising to his feet. "Can I fix you a drink?"

"Yes, please," I replied, shaking his hand. "I'll have one."

He began making a martini, which he made very well. "Your mother told Mrs. Taché about your arrest, Sunday, after Mass. We have been very concerned." He walked toward me, carrying a martini glass. "What evidence have they arrested you on?"

I listed the evidence and the reasons that the evidence did not fit. The one thing that I did not know, that was of most importance, was the date. There was no way I could clear myself of the crime without knowing when it took place.

Mrs. Taché, who had taken a seat by the fireplace, spoke. "It must be frustrating."

"Yes, ma'am, it is," I softly replied.

"God must have caused this for a reason," she said. She was a deeply religious woman, firmly believing in divine intervention. "He must be trying you for his purposes."

"He might be, but I wish he would let me know all of the facts," I responded. "This not knowing is making me a nervous wreck."

I pulled out a cigarette and lit it. The martini was dry. The day's cumulative alcohol was beginning to register upon my senses. If only I could suddenly be fully sober and find that the situation was a bad dream. We talked for several more minutes as I finished my drink.

"Well," I began, rising from the chair, "I really need to be going. There is someone else I must see tonight." I left the glass on the end table to my left.

"You don't have to leave so *soon*, do you?" Mrs. Taché pleaded.

"Yes. The past two days have been busy ones—as you can imagine—and there's still a lot I must get done before I leave tomorrow. I'll drop by before I leave."

"I hope so," she said.

"It's been good seeing you. Best of luck in Texas," Mr. Taché said, rising from his seat. We walked slowly to the front doors. "When do you leave?" he asked.

"The flight is scheduled for 6:20 tomorrow evening," I replied, turning my back to the door to face them.

"Well," Mr. Taché began, extending his hand to shake mine, "I guess I won't see you before you leave, then."

"No sir," I answered, slightly shaking my head. "I'll have to be leaving about 5:00 pm to get my ticket."

He grasped my hand. His handshake was strong and brief. "Things will turn out all right for you," he stated. "I am certain."

"Trust in the Lord," Mrs. Taché advised, putting her hand on my shoulder.

"I will," I said, before turning and twisting the doorknob. I had parked the Ambassador at the end of the walk that led directly to their front steps. As I walked around the front of the car, to the driver-side door on the opposite side, I looked back to the front door. The three were waving. I returned the wave and then opened the door and got in. The car was uneager to start, but finally growled in response to my threats of junking it. There was too much to do for me to be playing with the car.

Upon arriving at my parents', I quickly called Karen and told her I would be over as soon as I changed my clothes. She had wondered why I had not called her earlier, so I explained my visits that afternoon and evening. Changing clothes took virtually no time. I was anxious to see her. A hasty goodbye was shouted to my parents as I went down the stairs and through the door to the still-warm car.

It was drizzling as I drove to Karen's. The slow, rhythmic slapping of the windshield wipers took me temporarily out of attentive reality, as it had during the drive from the jail to the courthouse.

What are you doing, Mike? What does Karen mean to you? Are you that serious? If nothing developed in the almost seven years before this, why might something happen now? Yet there was something new to my feelings. They had never been this deep or frightening. *Could it be a yearning for some woman to genuinely love me?*

Whatever it was, it was confusing, fogging my ability to reason. Separating rational thought and actions from emotions was impossible. I found myself second-guessing responses to Karen—after I had acted. The trip to Texas would give me time to think rationally about us, sans her captivating, fogging influence. She was looking for a proposal from me, one that I was having difficulty envisioning. If I was going to make things final, there was no room for uncertainty.

The traffic light at the intersection of the road leading to Karen's required my attention and brought me back to reality. The area had changed so much since she first let me know that she liked me, those many years ago. These two roads had gone from one lane in each direction to three. What was once Kempsville farmland had become residential areas stretching for miles.

Karen was beautiful when she opened the door. She had curled her hair, which fell over her scarf and pastel blouse. The black slacks really accentuated her figure, as did her lace-up heels. A haze settled around my brain as I kissed her hello.

"How do I look?" she teasingly asked.

"Gorgeous!" I replied, taking off my coat.

"How soon did you want to leave?"

"It doesn't matter," I told her. "You are my only plans tonight."

"Miracle of miracles!" she sarcastically exclaimed in only a half-playful tone, looking at the ceiling.

"I haven't had much time since my release," I stated, a measure of irritation in my voice. "You're not the only person who is concerned about me."

"Nor am I the most *important*, am I?" she frankly retorted. The words were sharp and directed with a hurt look.

"Karen," I angrily replied, "that question is not at all fair." My teeth clenched, and what followed was spoken slowly and deliberately, as defining boundaries. "There are no grounds for comparison. They are important. Period!"

She hesitated, knowing she had angered me. "I'm sorry. You're right," she submitted, diverting her eyes.

The line of conversation had gone far enough. "Do you know of any good clubs around here?" I asked. "It's been a long time since I have gone dancing." My tone was conciliatory, offering a truce that I genuinely wanted.

"Let me think...." She pursed her lips in thought. "Oh yeah ... I know of one nearby that you'd like."

"Good. It should be a real good time."

"We're not going yet," she stated.

"We're not?" I asked, surprised.

"No. I bought something we're going to enjoy," she said as she fluidly moved into her kitchen. I trailed behind her. She opened the refrigerator and pulled out a bottle of wine. "You'll have to pop the cork," she told me, holding out the bottle to me. "I am not any good at it."

The cork came out with little effort, which was surprising because I was probably worse at pulling out the stupid things than she was. The wine was a tart Liebfraumilch, one of my favorites. Karen's intentions were obvious, yet I played willing donkey to her carrot. It took about an hour for much of the bottle's contents to disappear. She was becoming a bit giddy, and my reservations about standing my emotional ground were put into the refrigerator with the rest of the wine. I turned after closing the refrigerator door.

"Mike," she softly said, wrapping her arms around my neck, "I'll make you happy. You'll see."

There was no panic in my manner. The words were direct and honest, at least from her point of view. I allowed a moment to pass before speaking, trying to gain control of the conversation and guide it to something else.

"Why are you silent, Mike?" she asked, staring into my face. "Don't you think I can?"

"It's not that, Karen." I swallowed. "It's just that, with this criminal case looming over my head, I can't think of any future."

"Why not?" Her question was sharp. "You're going to prove your innocence."

"They seem to have a pretty good case against me," I answered.

She lowered her arms from around my neck. "That's not why you won't think about the future," she responded, her voice becoming critical. "Mike, I know you better than you know yourself."

She turned her head, looking out of the kitchen, and then looked back into my eyes. "You are afraid of admitting to yourself that you love me, or *anyone!*" Her tone was accusatory, indicting.

"That's not true!" I exclaimed, leaping to my defense.

"It is too!" she replied, her voice louder. "Try tearing down the walls you're building between us. If you spent as much time *tearing* down barriers as building them, we'd be *very* happy!" Her words were piercing. They hurt.

Her uncanny ability to see through me was unnerving, disturbing me. The truth of her argument bothered me. Not because I was dragging my feet and she could sense it, but because she was now— and had been for as long as I had known her—able to look right *through* me. A person must believe in the sanctity of his or her own thoughts, and around Karen mine were never safe. I did not respond to her challenge.

"Let's go on to that club you were talking about," I stated, determined to end my uncomfortable unmasking. "Where is your coat?"

Without speaking, she opened the closet by the front door and pulled out her coat, handing it to me. I helped her put it on, and we stepped through the door into a bitterly cold wind. The rain had stopped, but gusts blew through our protective garments, biting at our bodies. We practically ran to the refuge of my car, trying to escape the wind.

"Brrr ... it sure got cold in a hurry," Karen said as I got into my door, having seated her first. She shivered beneath her wind-strewn hair, pulling some strands away from the front of her face.

The light from the streetlamps made her moist eyes glisten. She was beautiful.

"We'll be warm in a minute, as soon as the car heater comes on."

"Why do we need to wait that long?" she asked, leaning across the seat to kiss me.

Her lips were soft, warm, and moist. After a long, tender kiss, I sighed and told her, "We're never going to get there if we keep this up."

"Okay. Okay," she replied with mock petulance, scooting back to her side of the bench seat. "Let's go."

The drive to the club only took minutes. Karen did not say anything on the way there, except when giving directions. My mind stepped out of the car and into the past, recalling the last time we had gone dancing, back in high school. It was the first time we had stopped seeing each other.

"What is the problem, Michael?" Karen had asked as we sat on the floor of the school gymnasium, the band blaring away in the background.

"I don't know how to say this, except to tell you," I began, looking into her face. "We need to start dating other people."

"*What?*" she angrily spouted. "*Why?*"

"We just do." I could not tell her she was overbearing, that she intimidated me, and I did not like feeling intimidated.

"You're mentally unstable!" she snapped back, rising to her feet. "You don't know what you want!"

"Maybe I don't," I stammered, "but maybe I do."

I had watched her angrily stomp away.

"Michael?"

"What?" I replied, startled, coming back to the present and the drive to the club.

"You're awfully quiet. What's wrong?" Karen asked.

"Nothing," I replied. "I'm just thinking."

"Oh no," she said in dismay, looking out the car passenger window as if something noticeable was occurring outside. There was a momentary silence. "Turn right, there," she stated, pointing ahead. "This is the place. We'll park in the back."

We hurried once more for respite from the wind, stepping from darkness outside into darkness inside. A hostess appeared from somewhere in the room, my eyes not yet accustomed to the light. "Could I show you to a table?"

"Yes, please," I replied.

The atmosphere was a blend of small pub hominess and disco glitter. The lighting consisted of large, softly glowing electric lanterns spaced one above each table. We were seated between the bar and the dance floor railing, away from the wall.

The waitress took our order and left. Karen began getting into the music's rhythm, her head swaying. The waitress returned with our drinks. Karen's eyes sparkled and crackled like fire as her head moved with the music. The lanterns dispersed around the room at different angles and in different intensities were reflected off her eyes.

She saw me watching her. She turned to me. "You know ..." she started, taking a sip of her bourbon and Seven, "we would have very beautiful children together."

Her statement did not upset me. I had thought about the children we might have. "They would be beautiful," I admitted.

"I want to have two children for you, Michael."

I took a sip from my drink. "Why only two?"

"Because ..." she replied, subdued, pausing. She lowered her head for a moment, raising it to look into my face. "I won't be able to have children in another four years. I've already had two operations for feminine problems." She looked up at the ceiling, her eyes watery.

"That's why you've wanted so badly to get married."

Karen looked at the floor, silently, then slowly nodded.

"I'm sorry," I offered.

"It's not your problem. Don't worry about it."

"Just knowing about it makes me feel bad, because I care about you," I replied, my voice slowing toward the statement's end, anchored to its truth.

"I'm sorry," she responded. "I thought you should know."

"Why don't we forget about it, for now? I'm not ready to ask you to marry me. I can't let what you told me affect my decision," I stated honestly.

Karen looked away, either unable or not wanting to reply. Words were not within my grasp.

The music that had earlier seemed to emanate from Karen's jubilant eyes now swallowed them with frustration. She'd bared the entire truth, and the extent of my response was not what she had wanted, much less hoped. She was playing for keeps. Now we both knew it.

The dancing was nice but anticlimactic in contrast to that discussion. She remained contented with my company, and we had a good time for a while. Men's eyes from around the room followed her movements. Karen was aware of it and ate up the attention.

"I don't know why I've kept waiting for you," she said, glancing over her shoulder at a nearby table. "There have been a lot of men who have wanted me for who I am."

"It's quite a bit more difficult for me than just wanting you, Karen," I replied, halting my scan of the décor to look at her. "You know how I feel about marriage. I have to be sure. You may think that I am, but I'm not."

"What is it about me that makes you so unsure?"

I did not want to discuss the matter but had invited the question, so I answered it. "You are, at times, a strong woman. Too strong." I paused. "For years ..." I began stammering, groping for subtlety. "You have—" No subtlety was to be found. "—intimidated me. I can't explain it any other way."

"Intimidated you," Karen said, sounding as if a statement. "I'm sorry," she indignantly began, "I did not want to *intimidate* you. I'm just trying to be myself. If you can't accept that, I apologize."

The song ended and we resumed our talk at the table. "Karen, I cannot get used to someone reading me like a book and telling me what I'm going to do before I even think about doing it." I glanced away from her, feeling exposed and vulnerable. Looking back, I told her, "If you were wrong more often, I suppose it would not bother me, but you are not wrong all that often."

Her response was quick and penetrating. "I know." She paused, as though gaining conviction. "I also know that you are not happy with yourself. Why are you so weak now? That's not the strength I know you have. You are so indecisive. Why?"

"I don't know," I meekly replied, looking at my clasped hands on the table. "I'm trying to be cautious, maybe too cautious." I nervously lit a cigarette, exhaled, and washed down the smoke with a sip of my drink. The waitress noticed my signaling her as I gestured for another round.

Returning to the unmasking, I turned back toward Karen. "It's just that I have been hurt . . ."

"*Hurt*?!" Karen exploded, cutting me off and drawing the stares of nearby tables. "You don't think that I have?" She took a swallow of courage. "For years you treated me like dirt."

"I apologized for that. I knew I was wrong."

"That doesn't make it any easier for me," she replied. "I've opened up completely to you, given you everything I possibly can give, and you still are not sure."

"Why?" I asked. "Why have you done it? I didn't ask you to."

"Didn't you? I thought I was over you for good when that letter came, just before Christmas." She paused. "I thought that you wanted to try again."

I was silent. Not getting a response, Karen asked, "Didn't you?"

"Yes," I humbly said.

"Well then *try!*" she burst out.

My mind was barren of thought. She had taken both sides of the discussion and left me the captive audience. The absence of spoken words hung around the table like a cloud of dust, choking any further intention on my part of speaking.

"You are too quiet," she said softly.

"I don't have anything more to say."

Karen asked for a cigarette. She did not smoke unless she was nervous. "Maybe you should take me home. It's getting late."

"Okay." I asked for the check and helped Karen with her coat. This time we walked slowly to the car, warmed by the argument and the liquor. We were quiet all the way to her house, neither of us daring to begin a conversation.

"I'm sorry we argued," Karen quietly said when we stopped in her driveway. "I had to tell you what was on my mind."

"That's all right," I replied in a conciliatory tone, knowing she felt the need to be completely honest.

"No, it's not," she said. "Now I've confused you even more," she said, looking at me and then turning to the window. "When do you leave for Texas?"

"The flight is at 6:20 at night. My father and I will be leaving about five o'clock."

"Then ... I won't get to see you until you return," she stated.

"I guess not," I replied, hesitating. "I hope I'll be able to come back," I added honestly.

"You will, dear," Karen said, placing her hand on my arm. "I have faith in you ... more than you have in me."

My window suddenly became interesting as I tried to avoid another confrontation. My not speaking disturbed Karen. She found her window interesting too, as I glanced toward her.

"Would you do me a favor?" she asked toward the window.

"What's that?" I replied.

Her head turned, her gaze now coming toward my face. "Would you come inside for a while? I don't know if I'll ever see you again."

The light hurt my eyes as I opened them. The clock on the wall said it was 8:45. Dragging myself from off the couch, I put on my clothes and went into the kitchen for some coffee. The morning was eternal unless I had my morning coffee.

"How was your date with Karen, last night?" Mom asked, drying her hands on a dishtowel to take a moment from her housework.

"It was okay," I replied, pouring a cup and then reaching for the sugar. "We went to a club and danced. We also talked quite a bit." I took a sip, pausing first to blow on the hot coffee. "I found out why Karen is so eager to get married."

"Oh? Why is that?"

"She has had female problems for years, and her doctors have told her that she'll be able to bear children for only a few more years."

"That's a terrible shame," my mother said with genuine sympathy.

"I told her, though, that I could not let that influence my decision. I thought I had better be honest with her."

"You really can't let it," she replied. "That would be unfair to you."

The coffee, hot and sweetened to taste, began waking up my body. There was so much to do today. Where was I to begin? "Are my clothes washed, Mom?"

"Yes, hon. They are on the table in the TV room."

We had not partitioned the laundry area from the rest of the room when we built the TV room. All cleaned clothes were folded and stacked on a table out of the viewing area. My mother liked it because she could do the laundry while watching her soap operas.

"Thanks, Mom," I replied. "I need to get packing."

"Yes," she stated, "you do."

I collected an assortment of shirts and pants from in the TV room and then went upstairs for one of my suitcases. I had never had to turn myself in before and did not know how to dress for such an auspicious occasion, I mused. The living room was a mess, covered with things not yet packed for my impending trip. The telephone rang in the kitchen. My mother picked it up, believing it to be one of her friends.

"Mike," Mom said from the kitchen, holding her palm over the receiver. "It's Karen."

I was surprised having her call this early in the day. I walked into the kitchen and took the receiver from my mother. "Hi, Karen."

"Good morning, hon," she softly said. "I didn't wake you, did I?"

"No, I've been up for half an hour. I was packing. What's up?"

"I was driving on the interstate," she began, her voice distressed, "to pick up a woman who rides with me to work. All of a sudden, the temperature light came on. I made it to her townhouse, but I'm afraid to try going to work, which is about fifteen miles from here."

"Okay," I replied. "Where are you now?"

Karen had stopped at some townhouses about a mile from my parents' home.

"All right. I'll be there shortly," I told her, and we said goodbye. I hung up the phone, shaking my head.

"What did Karen want?" Mom inquired, having entered the kitchen from the TV room after she heard me saying goodbye.

"She's having car problems," I explained. "It is overheating."

"She knows you have a lot to do," she snapped.

"I know. This should not take long. It is just up at Newtown."

"I hope not," Mom replied, returning to the TV room.

It did not take long. Her radiator was practically empty. She had a leak somewhere in her cooling system. I told her what to look for, had her get some water, and as she ran the engine I filled the radiator. All she said was thank you and good luck. She gave me a quick kiss and went back toward one of the townhouses.

My mother was curious about the episode when I returned. She frequently questioned Karen's actions, seeking ulterior motives. Maybe she thought I did not know how to see Karen through my emotions. Maybe she was right.

Packing took the remainder of the morning. I found a few dirty clothes, brought back from Texas, under a pile I had not previously sorted. My mother threw them into the washer and then looked at her watch.

"We need to go to the bank," she said. "Steve Paris said you will need expense money while you are in Houston. We can wire some money to his account and have you get it from him as you need it."

"Are you ready to go?" I asked.

"Not yet," she replied. "I have to change my clothes and brush my hair."

"Just let me know when you are ready," I told her.

Fifteen minutes later, we were at the bank. The funds transfer took very little time. We arrived back at the house about the same time Mike Haskett showed up. He cruised up in his 1955 Ford truck, for which he was known in our area. After unlocking the front door, I turned to speak to him. He opened the truck door, put on his signature reflective sunglasses, and then got out. Mike was an odd, friendly guy, almost childlike in his playfulness. His dark hair was parted down the center and tapered back to shoulder length. He had a little black mustache—or was trying to have one—and carried his waist, a remnant of good food and good beer, just above his belt.

"What's happenin', Crab?" he jested to me, catching up to us with long strides.

"I'm just getting ready," I told him, awaiting his entry. "Come on in," I said, shaking his hand.

"I planned on it," he replied. "How are you doin', Momma C?" he said to my mother. All of my mother's "adopted" children called her that. Mike had coined the nickname.

"Not much, Mike," she said. "Just getting him ready to go."

We walked inside. "What are you doing out of work?" I asked him.

"I'm out on a delivery, and eating lunch," he said. "I just came by to wish you luck."

"Thanks," I replied.

"Mike," Mom interjected, "would you like a sandwich?"

"Yes," Mike and I answered in unison.

Mike looked at me. "I said it *first*," he stated.

"No, you didn't," I replied, like a bratty kid, in the way he and I had kidded each other for the past several years.

"Do you want to fight?" he asked, grinning, playfully throwing a slow-motion roundhouse punch, which I blocked.

"You two stop playing!" Mom scolded. "I'll make some sandwiches."

We ate three sandwiches apiece, mine washed down with a beer and Mike's with milk. "It's too bad you can't have a cold one with me before I go," I smirked at him, knowing that he would have had he not been going back to work.

"That's all right," he replied. "I'll catch up to you tonight. You can *bet* on that! It's Quarter Night at the Firehouse Lounge. Draft beers are a quarter a glass."

"I guess you will," I said, laughing.

Having finished, Mike looked at me. "Well, bro'," he said, "I've got to go." He extended his hand. The look of concern on his face could not be disguised. "Good luck," he said.

"Thanks, Mike. I may need it," I told him, shaking his hand.

"Bye, Momma C!" he hollered to the TV room. "Thanks for the food!"

"You're welcome," came my mother's voice from the other room.

We walked out to his truck. He started it and slapped a tape into his eight-track player, mounted overhead. You could have heard the music inside the house. He bounced on the seat to the music's rhythm for a moment, said "see ya later," clutched it into first gear, and was off, merrily down the road.

"I'm going to visit a few people before I leave," I shouted to my mother as I entered the house, heading up the stairs.

"Okay," my mother replied. "Just be back before five o'clock."

I climbed the stairs and went into my parents' bedroom to use the phone.

Karen answered in a very professional tone. "Karen Stewart, may I help you?"

"I don't know," I replied. "Can you?"

"Oh, Mike. Are you packed?" she asked.

"Yes. All packed. I planned to go see some people this afternoon before leaving."

"Don't let me detain you," she said. "I'm sorry I called you this morning," she began. "I know you have a lot to do."

"That's okay. How did the car run?"

"It got hot again," she began. "I took it to a garage during my lunch break. The man said something about a head gasket."

"Uh oh!" I exclaimed.

"Is that real bad?"

"It could be," I replied, "depending upon how hot the engine got."

"Will it be expensive?" she nervously asked.

"That depends upon how hot it got," I answered.

"Oh, I guess so."

"Karen, I've got to be going," I stated.

"All right," she dejectedly replied. "Michael, you know I love you."

I paused. "I know," I told her.

"And you love me. You'll see," she replied, her voice confident.

"I'll talk to you later, Karen," I responded.

"Goodbye, Michael," she said, again dejectedly.

"Goodbye, Karen."

It was already after two o'clock. I still had to see the Tachés. I ran down the stairs, grabbed the car keys, and yelled "I'm going!" to my mother on my way out the front door.

Marianne, who had just gotten home from school, answered the door at the Tachés'. No one else was home. I left a message with her, for her parents and sister, Connie. Marianne looked at me, her face displaying sadness.

"Don't worry, Marianne," I told her. "It will be okay."

I left and drove down to Lynnhaven Inlet. A friend lived there on the beach. His little cottage was tucked between a hotel on one side and a condominium on the other. He had offers to buy the property for many years but did not want to give up his little haven by the water. I was glad he had not sold it. I had spent many peaceful days there, relaxing by the beach.

He was not home. Having made the drive, I decided to enjoy the view and tranquility for some time. I did not know when I might again get to visit. I walked down to the water's edge and just sat. Seagulls floated effortlessly in the breeze, changing directions with the flex of wingtips. The water gently lapped at the sand. A few boaters moved slowly through the inlet, on their way out to sea. Too soon, it was time to go. Although the same questions about the case and possible future arose in my mind, the water and scenery gave no resolution.

The drive back to the house seemed fast. When time was precious, it seemed to quicken as though denying being savored. I knew that the sensation was illusory, as my watch showed that the same time had been taken in returning as in going. My mind was racing the entire time.

Upon arrival, I collected my things and checked them against my list. All were here and ready. I showered, shaved, and dressed in a blue-gray suit.

Of the children, Paul was home, Joyce had not yet gone to work, and Barbara had just gotten home from track practice. Bobby and Cindy were still at work. I would not be able to see them before I left. Paul was in the kitchen talking with Mom when I came down the stairs carrying my shoulder bag.

I got a cold beer out of the refrigerator and gave him one too. He took the last swallow from the bottle that was already open in front of him. It clinked in the trash. He opened the one I had given him.

"Are you and Haskett going to the Firehouse Lounge tonight?" I asked him.

"Yeah, we're supposed to go. He's going to call me when he gets home from work," he replied, taking a sip.

"Do me a favor and tip one up for me. I'd rather be going with you to the Lounge than to Texas," I stated.

"We should be able to fit one into our tight schedule," he replied with a chuckle, smiling.

Barbara and Joyce came into the kitchen from the TV room. We smiled at each other. Theirs were uneasy smiles, tense. They seemed to be as nervous as I was. Barbara was always so undisturbed by everything that the little bit of nervousness she showed was very noticeable. Joyce's nervousness could have been seen from a mile away. She had always been an empathetic person.

"Are you nervous, Mike?" Joyce asked as she leaned against the refrigerator.

"Yes, I am," I stated honestly and frankly. "Wouldn't you be?"

She nodded in agreement.

"When are you supposed to arrive in Houston?" Barbara asked.

"Supposedly just a few minutes after eleven, but you never know," I replied.

"Make sure you call us when you get a hotel room," Mom said, busily preparing dinner. It would not be ready before I had to leave for the airport, but life could not come to a halt on my account. The rest of the family would be hungry after work and want something to eat.

"I've got to go, Mike," Joyce said. I stood up and she gave me a big, long hug. "Good luck," she told me, wiping the first tears from her eyes. "Everything will be all right."

"Thanks, Joyce," I replied. I heard the front door open and close. The three dogs hurried to the front door as they always did at five o'clock. Ending the hug, Joyce walked away toward the front door.

"Goodbye, Dad," I heard Joyce say on her way out. "See ya later."

"Are your things ready to go?" my father asked from by the front door.

"Yes, sir. Everything is ready to go," I answered.

"Go ahead and put it in the car," he instructed.

"Yes, sir." I carried the single suitcase to the car, returning to the kitchen.

Mom said to my father, "He's going to need some money, Wayne," who immediately took out his wallet.

"I know," he replied and began thumbing through bills in his wallet. "How much is plane fare, one way?" he asked.

"It's one hundred and thirty," I told him.

He returned his wallet to his pocket. "I'll go ahead and charge the ticket," he said. "I'll give you some money when we get to the airport." He drank a small cup of coffee and said, "We'd better get going."

Mom put down her cooking spoon and wiped her hands. She turned to me with tears in her eyes. "Good luck, Mike." She sniffled. "God will see you through this." We hugged each other very hard.

I turned, picked up my shoulder bag, and walked to the door. Barbara and Paul followed.

"Good luck," Paul said, shaking my hand.

"Thanks. Enjoy yourself tonight, but not too much," I told him. "Drink one for me."

"I will," he replied.

"Just be careful," I told him.

I turned to my baby sister. "Goodbye, Barb," I said. "Don't worry. Everything will be okay."

"I know," she responded, giving me a long hug.

I stepped away from our hug. Dad had already started the car and was waiting on me. I opened the car's back door, put in my shoulder bag, and then opened the front passenger door and sat down. Everyone waved from the front porch as we pulled away. It dawned on me that I might not see them for a long time. I did not wish to think about that.

I watched the scenery pass by the window. It would be difficult to board that airplane, although I knew it had to be done. The sun was right on the horizon. I found myself hoping it was not symbolic of my future.

The Difficult Journey to Houston

Dad broke the solitude of my thoughts as we headed down Military Highway toward the airport. "I want you to call tonight from Houston," he told me.

"Mom already told me to do that," I replied.

"I also want you to call any time anything new comes up."

"I'll do that," I said.

Nothing else was said on the way to the airport. We were heading into Norfolk, so the traffic was not bumper-to-bumper, as it was coming out of the city, toward the large residential areas of Virginia Beach. When we first moved into the area, almost twenty years back, Virginia Beach was a sleepy little suburb of Norfolk, covered almost entirely by farms. The population was around sixty thousand people. Today, the population of Virginia Beach was near or more than four hundred thousand, exceeding Norfolk's. The Hampton Roads area had grown to a population of more than a million.

I thought for a moment about something that my mother brought to my attention, earlier that day. The area had two major newspapers: *The Virginian-Pilot* and the *Ledger Star*, both very professional and giving extensive coverage to local matters. Four years before, ranked fourth academically in a high school class of more than eight hundred students, and lettering in five sports, I had been named "Outstanding Scholar-Athlete of the Year" for the area. My picture and a story had appeared in the newspaper. Now, however he did it, Sheriff Smith had kept the story of my arrest and extradition hearing *completely* out of both newspapers. My mother read the newspapers cover to cover every day. Nothing regarding my arrest made it to print. With the exception of those few persons whom we had informed, no one knew what was happening.

My father pulled to the curb at the ticketing area of the airport so that I could take out my bags. The suitcase was not overly heavy, just cumbersome. I got into the United Airlines tickets line while my father parked the car. By the time he came in, I was only a few customers from the counter. As my father stepped up to the available ticket agent, I placed my suitcase beside his position for check-in. The fellow's professional demeanor indicated that he had been in this line of work for some time.

"Do you wish to reserve a seat on a return flight?" the ticket agent asked.

Dad and I looked at each other momentarily, and then my father turned back to the ticket agent. "No, that will not be necessary at this time," he answered.

"Okay. Very well," the ticket agent replied. "You have the flight number, departure time, and gate number." He looked at us. "Correct?"

"That is correct," Dad replied.

"Have a very good flight, Mr. Crabtree," he said with a practiced smile. "Thank you for flying United."

There were still thirty-five minutes until boarding as we went up the escalator to the main level of the terminal. The boarding gates were down each of two long corridors that protruded from the main section of the single-building complex. The corridors formed a V shape, the apex away from the terminal.

"Do you want to have a beer or two at the lounge?" Dad asked. "There's plenty of time."

"Sure. Sounds good to me," I replied.

We walked into the lounge and sat at the table where I had sat the previous two times I had flown from Norfolk to Houston. Arriving early enough to make certain we had gotten to the airport in sufficient time, I had on previous trips stopped for a beer.

The familiar waitress approached our table. She must have had a rough day, as her face was haggard, weary. She feigned a smile. "Can I help you?" she asked, bringing her pen to a small pad in her left hand.

"Yes," Dad answered. "Two draft beers, please."

I lit a cigarette, which always seemed to go with a beer. Dad looked around the lounge at the different types of people in the room. The waitress returned with two large mugs of beer. "Will there be anything else?" she inquired.

"Not at the moment, thank you," I replied.

We each took a swallow of the sharp liquid. Dad seemed to have something to say. I could only sit there and wait for him to begin saying it. Dad never hurried his words, always choosing them carefully. He spoke only when he had something to say, and only when he had in mind how he was going to say it. His facial expression bothered me, so I tried to find something to steer his attention away from what he was contemplating.

"I like the outfits these waitresses wear," I said, pointing to an attractive waitress across the room. "Don't you?" I asked.

"They're not bad," he replied with a half-smile, as he glanced around.

I could tell that my weak attempt had been futile, as the look of concentration returned to his face. He took another sip, put down his mug, and turned his eyes to me. "I hope you learned something from this," he began.

"Yeah," I joked. "I learned not to drive beat-up old pickup trucks through small Texas towns."

He was not amused. "No, I'm *serious*," he replied, his voice firm. His look became stern. "You don't know how to handle the people that you have been hanging around with in Texas," he stated. "You blew all of the money you earned, didn't you?"

"Much of it," I meekly responded. "But that wasn't because of those people."

"What caused it?" he asked.

"Loneliness," I stated, taking a sip of beer before continuing. "Money can buy a pretty good time. When you're having a good time, you don't think about how lonely you are." I hesitated. "'Those people,' as you call them, were the only real friends I managed to make, because I was always traveling."

I glanced away for a moment. "It's tough making friends when you live in a tent, or when your home is simply an apartment you might go to for two days out of eight."

He studied me for a moment. "Were they your friends or your money's friends?" he asked.

"They were *my* friends!" I strongly replied. "I spent money on a few of them, helping them out."

"They didn't need a handout," Dad stated. "They don't look at it as help. They look at it as a freebee." He paused, looking more closely at me. "They begin looking *for* it, after a while." He took a swallow from his mug. "If you keep handing it out they will keep accepting, until you can't give, and then they turn their backs on you."

His comments made me uncomfortable; he did not know the people I had been associating with. A few had taken my money and run. Those were not long associated with me. I took another gulp of beer.

"How much did you shell out last year?" Dad asked.

"Oh, roughly fifteen hundred," I replied.

"Think how you could have used that," he stated. "Saving it would have done a whole lot more for you."

"You're right, Dad," I said in a surrendering tone, to end his sermon. He knew by my tone, and what I said, that his lecture was over.

"Do you really think that Kevin Silver could have set you up?" he asked, moving on to more important issues.

"I don't know, Dad. He might be capable of it, but I really can't say," I replied without conviction or status from which to make a warranted assertion.

I swallowed my last bit of beer. Dad downed his too, and then looked at his watch. "Would you like another?" he asked, in a way that let me know he wanted to be here with me.

"Yes, please," I replied.

He gestured to the waitress, who was already on her way over, having watched us empty our mugs. "Two more, please," he told her. He was silent, having said what he had to say.

"If the Texas police have nothing on me, I will sue the hell out of them!" I began, angry about the lack of even a basis for defending myself. "I mean it!"

Dad just stared at me, pondering.

"They can't do this to me without something to implicate me," I finished.

The waitress returned with two more mugs. We became silent in her presence, took a healthy swig, and resumed.

"Don't jump to conclusions," Dad replied. "There was probably something," he added, trying to calm me.

I lit another cigarette. My body felt like it was being sprayed with ice water. My hands were slightly trembling and my palms were wet and clammy. "I'm sorry," I told him, referring to my outburst. "I'm just nervous and scared, Dad."

"That's to be expected," he calmly observed. "Here is some spending money," he said, taking his wallet out of his pocket. He counted off amounts as he pulled bills. "Seventy dollars should cover everything until you can see Mr. Paris tomorrow morning." He handed me the money, which I immediately tucked into my own wallet. "You have his address and directions, don't you?"

"Yes, sir," I replied. "Right here in my bag."

"Good." He looked at his watch and then picked up his mug. "We'd better be going," he stated, looking at me. "It's about time to begin boarding."

We downed the beers. Dad called for the bill, left some money, and joined me. I had already walked to the lounge exit. The walk to the entrance of the gates corridor seemed to take but a few seconds. I was trying to hold on to the last minutes here.

"You'd better be going," Dad told me.

"Yeah, I guess so," I solemnly replied.

He hugged me, and stepped back to shake my hand. "Good luck, son," he said.

"Thanks, Dad." My words were not enough to fight the fear welling in me. What could be said? No words could change this.

"Call us," he instructed me.

"I will."

With that, I turned and walked down the corridor. My bag was x-rayed as I went through the metal detector. The security guard's cold eyes followed me for a moment as I walked on toward my gate. Arriving at the gate, I chose a seat far from the door. A newspaper was lying beside the chair I had chosen. No sooner had I picked it up than the attendant announced that boarding was to begin.

"This is it," I said to myself. "Goodbye, Norfolk. I hope to see you again soon."

I shouldered my bag, walked numbly down the ramp to the jet, and took my seat. My mood was as dark as the evening now covering the city. It was not long before the plane was pushed from the gate, taxiing to the runway. My face was transfixed to the window. The engines grew loud. We began to roll. The light posts beside the runway passed by faster and faster, and we were in the air.

The city's lights were pretty. Streams of red taillights filled the streets, countered by white headlights streaming the other ways. I looked below, trying to see my neighborhood as the aircraft headed southwest. When would I see it next? We eventually passed from the suburban area and the ground below became darkness, spotted by occasional lights over the countryside.

In Atlanta, the faces watched me exit the ramp as I came from the jet into the terminal. People in the departure area were eagerly awaiting their chance to board and join the continuing flight onward to New Orleans. Atlanta was as damp as it was cold, and I was glad that the walk from aircraft to the terminal was short. Advertisements on the walls seemed to stare at me. This was getting more difficult by the step, and my pace was slowing. There was a telephone on the wall opposite of the boarding ramp. It was an oasis from this temporary paranoia.

"Hello," someone answered.

"Hello, Mom?" I stammered. "I'm in Atlanta."

"How was your flight?" she asked.

"Not too bad," I replied. My voice lowered in pitch, the sound of a familiar voice relieving the nerves that tried to strangle me.

The meal on the flight from Norfolk had been a good one, as far as airline meals go. Following the meal, I took time from my nervousness to give in to fatigue. The fact that there was no turning back allowed me to relax, even if temporarily. The stewardess had awakened me a few minutes before the landing. I had fastened my seatbelt so I could go back to sleep, but the lights of suburban Atlanta kept my eyes occupied. Much like Norfolk's, the Atlanta streets looked like thousands of Christmas light strings weaving their way through gray channels, crisscrossing, flowing, moving almost imperceptibly. The plane had made a sharp right bank and begun its final approach.

"Well, be sure to call us from the hotel in Houston," Mom told me.

"I will. I'll talk to you later," I said.

"Okay. Bye," she replied.

"Goodbye, Mom," I said back, and then the sound was a click and nothing. I looked at the receiver for a moment before placing it back on the pay phone box.

My steps were sure and directed. The lounge in this terminal was a very classy one, with good drinks and service. Entering, I took a seat at a table in a corner; I felt most comfortable being able to look at everyone in the bar. The room was dimly lit. People of all classes were present. Most were businessmen, drinking and conversing between glances at their watches.

"Could I get you something?" the attractive brunette waitress asked.

"Yes. A Seven and Seven, please," I replied.

She walked by a table of men with cowboy hats, denims, and pointed-toed boots, taking their order before going to the bar. *Karen would like this place*, I thought. It was classy.

My thoughts turned to her. Seven years was a long time. Most of the time had been spent apart, because of my wishes. Twice in the period I had contemplated marriage to other women, most recently to Anna. Karen had continued to hope that I would come back to her. Time after time I had.

"Here ya go," the waitress said, placing the drink in front of me on the table. "That will be a dollar seventy-five."

"Thank you," I said, handing her a ten.

"I'll be right back with your change." She turned and headed to the cash register. I watched her walk away.

My watch told me I had fifteen minutes to reserve a seat prior to boarding. I did not want to fly to Houston. I wished I had had a choice in the matter. I held the glass loosely in one hand, tapping a finger against it with the other.

"Here is your change," the waitress said, surprising me, as I was engrossed in thought. She placed a tray of bills and coins on the table and then moved on to another table.

"My compliments to the bartender," I quietly said to myself after tasting the drink. The next few minutes sort of dissolved away, as I did not notice their passing. I looked at my watch again, and there were only ten minutes until boarding. The glass was half-empty, not half-full. I drank it quickly, placed a tip by the empty glass, and stood up, throwing the bag's strap over my shoulder.

The steps were less certain. People-to-people carpeting moved perpetually through the terminal. I stepped into the flow and was at my Delta Airlines departure gate four minutes before boarding. The gate attendant took my ticket.

"Smoking or non-smoking, Mr. Crabtree?" he asked.

"Smoking."

"There is one seat left, on the aisle," he replied.

"That is fine," I responded.

"Very well; seat seventeen C, aisle. Have a good flight, Mr. Crabtree," he said, handing me a boarding pass and a folder to put the ticket in. "Hand the boarding pass to the flight attendant as you board."

Saying "thank you," I turned and looked for a seat. There was a stunning blonde woman in a beautiful pink dress facing the ticket counter, in the nearest seats. She looked up at me. I just briefly grinned in acknowledgment. In a corner of the room to my right was an empty seat. I did not get to sit. The boarding call interrupted my walk to the chair.

As I found my seat on the airplane, I also found that the blonde woman was seated across the aisle from me. The stewardesses gave their emergency procedures presentation and the jet rose into the Georgian skies.

The flight to Houston was to take approximately eighty minutes. The No Smoking light went out, so I lit one. The blonde, a buxom woman, probably in her early twenties, pulled a magazine out of the travel bag she had put under the seat in front of her. She was trying to read it, but she had not turned on the reading light on the overhead console.

"Excuse me, Miss," I said to her. "It might help your eyes if you turned on your light."

"That's true," she said with a short giggle. "I should have thought of that." She reached up, turned on her light, and then reached back into the travel bag beneath the seat. "Would you like a magazine?" she offered.

"Yes, please," I replied. I accepted the magazine, turned down the portable tray from the seat back in front of me, and began flipping through some pages.

"It might help if you turned on the light," she suggested, grinning.

"Oh, yeah," I said, chuckling. "I should have thought of that." We laughed. "Thank you," I added, having switched on the light. I scanned the index for a moment, and then turned to an article.

"Do you have a light?" the woman asked.

"Sure," I replied, trying to reach into my suit's breast pocket. I lit her cigarette.

"Thank you," she said after exhaling.

"You're welcome."

She looked back at her magazine, for just a minute, before closing it. "My name is Pam," she told me.

"I'm Mike," I replied. "It's nice to meet you."

"Where are you from?" she asked.

"I'm from Virginia, originally. I've been living in Houston for the past year."

"*Really?*" she responded. "What part of town?"

"Southwest Houston," I began. "I'm living in some apartments by Fondren, on Main Street."

"I'm not far from there," she replied. "My apartment is between Richmond and Westheimer."

"I know where that is," I told her. "It's only about five miles away from me." I closed the magazine. "How long have you lived in Houston?"

"Since May. I'm working at a hospital in the Texas Medical Center complex. I finished nursing school in Indiana and came to the city with a girlfriend, to go to work."

"I've been working in the oilfield," I informed her, "traveling around the state. Houston is just my mailing address." I paused. "Perhaps I can look you up when I'm in town on my days off."

"Perhaps you can," she replied. She was quiet for a few seconds. "I was supposed to have already arrived in Houston, but the Chicago Airport was snowed in."

"I heard about that," I told her.

"They rerouted me from Indiana through the East Coast. This is my *fifth* flight today," she exasperatedly said.

"That's *terrible*," I replied. "Were you visiting relatives in Indiana?"

"Yes. I'm supposed to begin a job at another hospital on Monday," Pam began. "I took a vacation after leaving my last job. I hadn't had one since I began working."

"Oh, I see," I replied.

"Are you flying from Virginia?" she asked.

"Yes," I said. "I left my job last month, having put away money to go back to school." I hesitated for a moment, not knowing if I should say more, but decided to go on. "Why I'm returning is a different story, and a very long one," I stated.

"I've got time," she replied. "I'm not going anywhere," she added, quietly giggling. "Go ahead."

"Well … it's like this," I started. I told her the story in condensed form. She listened intently. I could not tell if she believed me. Her gaze did not leave my face the entire time. Her eyes were bright green, shallowly set in a rounded face with high, full cheeks. The long, thick lips moved at my story's conclusion.

"Wow!" she replied. "That's something else!"

I just nodded in agreement before turning my head, catching the look of astonishment on the lady seated directly behind Pam. I leaned toward Pam and then she leaned toward me. "She must think it is, too," I whispered to her, pointing with my thumb and a pivot of my hand toward the lady behind her.

Pam turned and looked at the middle-aged woman. We chuckled for a moment. Pam said, "She must be flipping out. Not everyone rides on a plane with a fellow talking about turning himself in for an armed robbery." Pam laughed.

"You believe me, don't you?" I asked.

"Yes, I do. You have an honest face," she replied.

"Thank you. I just hope I can get this cleared up quickly," I told her.

"So do I. That's *terrible*. They said it was your truck?" she asked.

"That's what they say. I don't think it was but can't prove it yet," I stated.

"Wow!" she responded, shaking her head.

The stewardess stopped in the aisle with her beverage cart. "Can I get you something to drink?" she asked me.

"Yes, please," I told her. "Pam, would you like one?"

"Yes," she answered.

"I'll have a Seven and Seven," I told the stewardess.

"We don't have any Seagram's Seven, but we do have V.O.," she said.

"That will be fine," I replied. "What would you like, Pam?"

"That sounds good to me," she said.

The stewardess handed us the tiny bottles of V.O., two cups, and 7-Up.

"Cheers!" I said to Pam. The stewardess resumed her service, rolling the cart down the aisle.

"To continue," I said to Pam, "my attorney in Houston told me not to stay in the apartment, because Kevin lives in the same complex. Until this is cleared up, I will be staying in hotels."

"I could give you a ride," Pam told me. "There is a Holiday Inn on the 610 Loop, by where I live."

"Thank you," I replied. "That would be nice."

"I just hope my roommate, Janet, is at the airport when we arrive," she said.

"Is she expecting you?" I asked.

"Yes, but at nine o'clock. She might have given up and gone home," she surmised.

"I hope not," I replied.

"So do I," Pam said.

"What are you going to do if she's not there?" I asked.

"I'll call the apartment. She would probably go back there and wait for my call."

We talked for a few more minutes. Pam had two siblings, both older. She said "wow" again when I told her my family had six kids. We traded stories, laughing. She told me about Fort Wayne, her home. In time, and a round of drinks later, I was feeling very comfortable. "I'm glad that I met you, Pam," I told her.

"It's mutual," she replied.

I pulled out the magazine and returned to the article I had begun reading. I lost track of my reading as I thought about calling my parents after my Houston arrival. That brought me back to the case. I reached into the bag I had placed under the seat in front of me, retrieving the envelope labeled "State of Texas vs. Michael W. Crabtree."

Sorting through its contents, I wasn't quite sure what I was seeking. Consequently, I didn't find it. I read through my notes and jotted down some more questions for Mr. Paris. "God, help me through this," I said to myself. I took another sip, put all of the contents back into the envelope, and put it away.

"May I have your attention, ladies and gentlemen," the pilot announced over the intercom. "We'll be making one more flight correction for our descent to the Houston Intercontinental Airport. If you have not fastened your seat belt ..."

I fastened my belt and then took out a cigarette. "It looks like this is it," I told Pam. "I hope Janet is there."

"Me, too," she replied.

I lit my cigarette and hers. We were able to smoke only half of each before the No Smoking light came on.

The landing was uneventful. The Welcome to Houston sign greeted us as we entered the boarding ramp. The Houston terminal was very well lit: a new, modern structure.

"I'm going to go find Janet as soon as possible," Pam informed me as we left the gate.

"I'll pick up your luggage if you'd like," I told her.

"Thank you," she replied. She described her suitcases and handed me the claim stubs.

By the time she returned, I had retrieved our luggage.

"Did you find Janet?" I asked.

"No," she said with a frown. "She wasn't at the apartment either. She must have thought I would be in tomorrow."

"I hope not. Maybe you could call her after a while," I said.

"Maybe so," she replied.

I took her largest suitcase and my own, and we left the baggage claim area. "We have some time to waste," I said. "Would you like to go to the lounge?"

"Yes, I think I would," she replied. "Where can we put these?" she asked, about the luggage.

"There is a security guard by the lounge entrance," I told her. "We can leave them in his sight."

"Sounds good to me," she answered with grin.

"Okay then," I replied. "It's a date."

We dropped off the luggage and entered the lounge. The security guard by the door said he would keep an eye on our things. A waitress showed us to a table, and I held the chair for Pam as she was seated.

"Two Seven and Sevens," I told the waitress. "Right?" I asked Pam.

"Yes, please," she replied.

"How soon did you want to call Janet again?" I asked her as the waitress left.

"In about fifteen minutes or so," she said. "What time is it?"

I looked at my watch, which read twelve thirty, and then at a clock on the wall behind the bartender, which showed eleven thirty-five. "I forgot to set my watch back," I told Pam. "It's eleven-thirty."

"Where did you get that watch?" she asked, grasping my wrist to get a better look.

"I got it for playing in the Peach Bowl, in Atlanta, in college," I began. "I played football in college for two years."

"It's pretty," she said. "Why did you quit?"

"Many reasons," I replied. "Mainly because of a back injury. I broke a bone in my back, in practice, pinching a nerve to my leg, and had no muscle control of the leg for a couple of days."

"I'll bet you were scared."

"That is an understatement," I said. "They later told me that another collision could lead to permanent paralysis, so I gave it up."

I was always a very open person, but I found it extremely easy to talk to Pam. She was a warm, receptive person, probably very good as a nurse. Her manner was charming, but not in an affected way. She was naturally emotive, with subtle gestures emphasizing statements during her talking. She smiled quite a bit, the corners of her lips seeming to assume a happy or placid anticipation as though predisposed. She was charming and disarming. She laughed easily and genuinely. Her eyes sparkled. We sat, discussing many things over drinks, and making occasional calls to her apartment, until the lounge closed at one o'clock.

"What do you want to do?" I asked Pam.

"I don't know," she said, her concern apparent in her voice. "It's not like Janet to be out like this. I'm getting worried about her."

"We could take a bus into town, and from the station catch a cab to your apartment," I suggested.

"That is a good idea," she responded.

"You go ahead and call again," I said. "I'll carry the baggage to the bus curb."

We waited near the curb for thirty minutes, running in and out of the terminal at the approach of each bus. They were running off schedule, so we did not know which one would be ours. The bus took us through the downtown area on the loop it made before returning to the airport. The downtown area was well lit, its mostly one-way streets almost empty of traffic. Skyscrapers rose from shadows upon the sidewalks and seemed to end at the edge of darkness and stars. Streetlights reflected off of the glass windows and polished façades, making the area seem livelier than it was in the quiet night.

We got off on one of the last stops, a small terminal on Richmond Avenue, by the Galleria. Pam had taken my hand during the trip. It seemed almost natural, a very relaxed and unpretentious gesture of being comfortable with me. For much of the time, she slept with her head on my shoulder. Her breathing had been slow and barely audible in the now-empty bus, except for us and the driver. It touched me that she could come to so trust me so quickly. Her hair smelled nice. Her perfume's fragrance was soft, not overpowering and not too sweet. It was feminine without being overbearing. She was causing me to rethink my situation with Karen.

"Hello, Mom?" I asked into the receiver.

"Yes," she replied, her voice rough with sleep.

"I was delayed at the airport," I began. "I met a girl named Pam while flying here from Atlanta. She is going to give me a ride to the Holiday Inn, nearby."

"Where are you?" she asked.

"I'm at a bus terminal near the hotel. We just got here."

"I don't know if it is a good idea for you to be getting a ride from her this late at night," Mom replied, being Mom.

"Why not?" I asked, surprised.

"She could rip her clothes and start yelling 'rape,'" she stated.

"She wouldn't do that, Mom," I emphatically replied. "She is a very nice girl."

"Still," she responded, "you're in enough trouble already. You don't need to take any chances."

"Okay, Mom," I told her. "I'll call you tomorrow and give you my address and phone number."

"All right. I'll be expecting it," she stated.

"Goodnight, Mom," I said.

"Goodnight."

I turned to face Pam. "What was that about?" Pam asked.

"My mother," I explained, "is afraid that you'll start yelling 'rape,' or something. She doesn't want me to accept a ride from you. She is just paranoid."

"I wouldn't do that," she stated.

"I know you wouldn't, but my mother doesn't. I'd still like that ride."

Pam smiled. "That's good," she said.

I hailed a taxi and we rode the mile or so to Pam's apartment. We transferred the luggage to her brown Buick before going into the apartment. Janet was not home when we entered. The apartment was nicely furnished, clean.

"Would you like some coffee?" Pam asked.

"Yes. That would do me a lot of good," I replied.

"Me too," she said. "It will only take a minute."

The hot coffee was good. It was now after three, and my body was trying to go to sleep. Pam was still concerned about Janet, and we briefly talked. Pam's car took some time to start, not having been run in weeks. The journey to the hotel took only a few minutes.

The clerk did not seem surprised when I requested a single room that late at night, with a beautiful blonde sitting behind the wheel of the car, in plain view. He looked out at Pam, back at me, raised his eyebrows, and then continued with his register entries. I grinned at him, amused with his incorrect preconception. Neither she nor I were like that. We drove around back, to my room. I set my suitcase down at the door and returned to the car.

"I want to thank you for a wonderful, if not unusual evening," I told her through her open window.

"I had a really good time, too," she replied, a large smile on her face.

"You know," I began, "when I saw you in Atlanta, I wanted to meet you. It was my good luck to sit across from you on the flight."

Pam responded, "I wanted to meet you. I didn't read the magazine in the dark on purpose, but I'm glad I did."

"I had to start a conversation somehow," I replied, grinning. "That just gave me an opportunity."

"You're a real nice person, Mike," Pam said. "I'm glad I met you." Her eyes reflected the streetlight behind me, making them shine in contrast with the interior of her car and the pale blue-gray appearance of her cheeks.

"I'd like to see you again," I said hopefully.

"I'd like that," she replied.

"I'll probably be changing hotels tomorrow," I told her. "My attorney will want me close to his office. Do you know where Texas Avenue and Caroline are?"

"I'm not sure," she answered. "I think they're downtown."

"I'll need your phone number so I can contact you."

"Okay," she replied, giving me the number. "Can you remember that?"

"I'll write it down in a minute. Thanks again," I told her. I leaned in the window and kissed her on the cheek. "Goodnight," I said.

"Goodnight."

I stood up and stepped back from the car, which pulled away into the night. I watched until it passed from sight and then turned to enter the room.

The hotel room was nice. There was a round table and two chairs near the front of the room, close to the wall-mounted air conditioner. There was a pad of paper and a pen on the nightstand by the bed. I walked to the nightstand, turned on the light, and wrote down Pam's number. It was too late to think about anything, so I called the wakeup service, got undressed, and turned out the light. It was just after four o'clock. Tomorrow's experience would arrive in only a few hours, whatever it would bring.

Prelude to Unknown Future

R-r-r-ring. I turned over. R-r-r-ring. I turned the other way. I knew the phone was ringing, but I was too tired. R-r-r-ring.

"Hello," I softly said.

"Good morning. It is nine o'clock," the voice told me.

"Thank you," I replied.

I showered and got ready very quickly, and then went for a few cups of coffee. My mother answered when I called from a pay phone, informing her I was about to leave for Mr. Paris's office. I returned to the room, called the front desk to get a cab, and closed my suitcase. It was ten o'clock.

The ride to Mr. Paris's office would probably take half an hour, I guessed. I was in a hurry to find out what information had been gained from the Colorado County police. I was also wondering if any additional evidence had been introduced. The most important datum was still the crime's date.

The cab did not arrive until 10:30. The weather was cold and steadily drizzling. I put my suitcase into the trunk, got into the back seat, and the driver took off as if trying to outrace time. I wondered how he drove when he was late and *knew* it. We arrived five minutes late.

Mr. Paris's office was in a modern, marble building downtown. I walked into the front doors carrying my bags, accompanied by the stares of passersby. The directory of the building was immediately in front of me, but was unnecessary. The Evans and Paris office was directly to my left, behind a large, ornate hardwood door, surrounded by translucent, detailed glasswork. I placed the bags in the lobby, by the door, and went in.

I sat down on a couch by the door. Before me sat the sweet southern drawl, I surmised; an attractive and competent receptionist like one out of a movie. "May I help you?" she asked. Definitely the Texan I talked to on the telephone, I knew.

"Yes. I'm Michael Crabtree. I was to see Mr. Paris at 11:00."

"Of course, Mr. Crabtree," she said. "Mr. Paris is with another client at the moment. Would you like a cup of coffee?"

"Yes," I replied. She rose from behind her desk. I stood to hang up my coat.

"I'll get it," she told me.

"I was just going to hang up my coat," I told her, grinning at her misunderstanding.

"Oh," she replied.

"That's okay. Make that one sugar, please," I said.

"Will do," she replied.

She walked into a room that was empty with the exception of a photocopier and a table covered with a coffee percolator and the additives. Her hair was long and dark, resting daintily on her petite but padded shoulders. She was wearing a green, well-tailored dress that came to her knees. "My name is Sharon," she told me from the other room.

"It's nice to meet you," I replied.

She returned with a steaming cup in a plastic holder. "Oh, David," she said to a red-haired man who was approaching from the office hall. "I'd like you to meet Michael Crabtree."

I rose from my chair to accept the coffee from Sharon with my left hand and to shake David's hand with the right one. He was in his early twenties, I guessed, although he appeared younger: the small frame glasses and freckles suggested a college freshman. His voice was firm and commanding respect.

"Mr. Crabtree, my name is David," he told me, his handshake firm, concise. "I work for Mr. Paris."

"Please," I told him, "call me Mike." I looked at Sharon. "You too, Sharon." She nodded as she typed.

"Okay," David replied, "I will. I know only a little bit about your case. Tell me some more about it." He sat on the plush chair to the right of the couch.

I sat on the couch, setting the coffee on the end table between us. I began briefly describing the case as I perceived it, pointing to the importance of the crime's date. David sat silently for a moment.

"This," he began, unconsciously playing with his pen, "has been an extremely unusual case." He looked me in the eyes. "We have not been able to gain much information, I'm afraid. They have had some kind of communication problem over there. It seems as though the man in charge of the investigation has been sick. No one else knew about the case."

"I don't believe that," I said, frustrated. "There was no crime report? No filed reports or affidavits?"

"Nobody had them on hand," he replied, subdued. "I wish we could have helped you more."

"You can't help me if the police will not talk to you," I frankly told him. "I hope we have better luck the rest of the way."

"I am sure we will. You are supposed to talk to them next week," he informed me.

I numbly nodded, in thought. *Should I be glad? Hopefully, I can get to the bottom of this then. How will they treat me?* "Will Mr. Paris be going with me?" I asked David.

"Yes, he will," he replied. "He will be driving you there."

"That's a relief," I stated. There was an ashtray on the table. I pulled the cigarette pack from my shirt pocket, gesturing as if asking whether smoking would be acceptable.

"Sure," David told me.

I lit a cigarette, my nervousness increasing with proximity to the Columbus trip. I was so certain Mr. Paris and his associates would have found something new prior to my arrival. This conversation had left me no closer to the truth.

A handsome man in his early thirties, with sandy hair and gold-rimmed glasses, stepped from an office, very neatly attired in a light gray striped suit. He said a quick hello in my direction, gave Sharon a set of papers, and retired to another room down the hall. "Who was that?" I asked.

David turned back to face me, his eyes also having followed the man. "That," he said, "was Mr. Evans, Mr. Paris's partner." David stood up, and I rose with him. "Mr. Paris should be finished in a few minutes," he told me. "It was a pleasure meeting you, Mike."

Once again, I accepted his firm but brief handshake. "It was a pleasure meeting you, David."

"If I can be of any help," he said, his arms akimbo, "or answer any questions that you might have, feel free to call me."

"Thank you. I will do that," I replied.

David turned and walked to the room into which Mr. Evans had gone. I sat down. Sharon typed with only her fingers moving, resembling a manikin with animated hands.

The table by the couch was covered with periodicals of all kinds. I picked one up and browsed through it. I was thinking too much to be distracted by my eyes. Instead of gaining answers, I was stockpiling questions unable to be answered.

"Sharon," the intercom squawked, "please send Mr. Crabtree in."

"Okay, Steve," Sharon replied. "Mike, you can go in now."

"Thank you," I said. I put out my cigarette in the ashtray, walked to the door, and knocked.

"Come in."

The door opened into a light green room, wallpapered with framed certificates. A magnificent oak desk consumed most of the floor space. There were two chairs facing the desk and Mr. Paris's "throne"—a huge, brown leather upholstered chair. He concluded a telephone conversation and looked up.

"Please have a seat," he told me, getting up and walking toward me. He was thirty-something, tall, and of average build, with straight chestnut hair, dark eyes, and the beginnings of a full beard. "My name is Steve Paris," he said.

"I'm Mike Crabtree," I replied, shaking his hand. "Please call me Mike."

"I will. Call me Steve."

"Okay," I replied.

"I'm going to ask you something," Steve began. "The way in which I represent you will depend upon your answer." He returned to his chair and peered over his immense desk. "I know what you have told your father. I want you to be honest with me." He leaned across the desk, his elbows resting on a large desk pad. "Did you rob that store, or have any knowledge of the robbery prior to your arrest?" He paused, his eyes pinning me to my chair.

"No, Steve," I stated firmly. "I knew nothing of the robbery before my arrest."

"I believe you, Mike," he said, leaning back into his chair. "The reason I ask is because 90 percent of the people I represent are guilty. Assuming you are innocent, I will represent your case differently than I would if you had told me you were guilty. If you were guilty, I would not take you to Columbus. I would not allow them to talk directly to you. I would force them to prove your guilt. Taking you to them could cause you to make a mistake in your story. Since you tell me you are innocent...." He paused for a moment. "You still want me to represent you in that manner?"

"*Yes*," I emphatically stated. "I have nothing to hide. I am innocent," I frankly told him.

"All right," he said, "we will go to see the Columbus police on Monday." He glanced at a piece of paper on the desk in front of him, picking it up. "We are to see Captain Brooks that afternoon. He and ... Chief Teoson," he said, reading from the paper, "of the Weimar Police Department will be there to question you."

I nodded in approval.

"I will be there to represent you, read any documents they may want you to sign, and in general make sure your rights are not violated." With that, he seemed to have finished.

"What information have you been able to gather?" I asked him.

"The police are not telling me anything new," he replied. "This has been one of the worst handled cases I have come up against. The Colorado County police seem like a bunch of simpletons. No one, except this Captain Brooks, claims any knowledge of details of the crime. He has been sick for the past three days, or so their desk clerk told me."

"They had better have some kind of case against me," I angrily said. "If they do not, I will do everything in my power to sue them."

"It is too early to say anything about a lawsuit. Suing the police is tricky business. Let's not talk about it now," Steve explained without excitement.

"If you say so," I quietly replied.

Mr. Paris spent the next twenty minutes going over the case. We both took notes: I of his questions and him my responses. He tried to give me some idea what the police would ask and which questions I could avoid answering, if the line of questioning got too tight.

"All I need to know is the date of the crime," I again told him. "Over the four days I spent in jail, I mentally covered the entire first two weeks of December. The only thing I lack—the key to my defense—is the date. When I know that, I will know where I was that day, and how to prove it." I felt that he understood: getting that date, it would all be over.

"What do you know about this ..."—He looked at a piece of paper—"Kevin Silver?"

I told him I had no way of implicating Kevin, although I thought he was capable of it, had he been desperate enough.

"We cannot prove that Silver had anything to do with the crime, but it might give them something to think about," he informed me. He continued taking his notes, his left hand continually moving his pen. His momentary silence allowed me to study the array of accolades and certifications adorning his walls.

"Do you have any other questions?" I asked him.

"No," he replied. "I will contact Columbus Monday morning. Be here at 1:00." He rose from his throne. "Where are you staying?"

"I spent last night in a Holiday Inn on the 610 Loop, but I brought my baggage. I checked out of that hotel this morning."

"Good," he stated. "There is a hotel down Texas Avenue," he said, "about a block from here. If you stay there, you will be within walking distance of my office." He paused. "Is there anything else?"

"Oh," I remembered, "I'm going to need some expense money. My father gave me enough to last until I saw you today."

"Talk to Sharon," he replied. "We will just deduct it from the amount your parents deposited in the company's account." He walked from behind his desk, and I rose to meet him. "Call us Monday morning," he stated. "Until then, stay near your hotel room." We shook hands. "I will see you then."

Sharon wrote me a check, which I cashed at the bank next door. I picked up my bags and rejoined the rain. The looks of busy Houstonians searched me as I strode toward the hotel. The television would entertain me after I got a bite to eat.

The fifth-floor room's balcony afforded a view of the bustling activity on the ground below. The gloomy drizzle gave the surrounding area a gray tint, as impersonal as the synchronized traffic lights on the one-way downtown streets. Cars darted in and out of lanes, among one another, as though playing a game of tag where contact was to be avoided.

The street was almost musical: a cacophony composed of horns, screeching tires, and changing engine speeds to the rhythm of windshield wipers and temporary taillight colors. The pedestrian audience was restless, continually traversing the sidewalks and crosswalks. They, too, followed the rhythms of the light show at the corners. Taking a break from the concert outside, I called Virginia.

Pam would be home at three-thirty. I hoped she was not busy, because I wanted to take her to dinner. *How much do I feel for Karen, if it is easy to put her out of my mind? Why did I care so much when I was around her but could forget her when I was away from her? Am I trying to lead her on, or was I leading myself on?* "I guess you'll have to give yourself time," I quietly said, no one else around to hear.

Unpacking took little time. I did not bring much clothing. Boredom stared me in the face, no matter which way I looked, so I went to sleep.

Later, Pam said she did not have any plans and would be glad to pick me up. It would be interesting to be picked up for a date. It had been a long time since I had someone drive me to a date. I thought back. Karen was the first girl to drive me to a date, as she had her license and I was not yet old enough to get one. My mother did not know what to think at the time, her son getting a ride from this willful girl a year older than him.

"Ah, Mom, please?" I could still see that discussion in my memory.

I was excited as the time approached for Pam to arrive. She was punctual, her arrival a gentle rap on the door. She was beautiful as I opened the door, more beautiful than I had really noticed the previous night. Her lips glistened in the light. Her eyes smiled at mine.

"You look *fantastic*," I told her, holding the doorknob as if it was going to fall off.

"Thank you," she said, still standing in the cold breezeway. She smiled, looked inside, and then back at me. "Are we going to leave now or just stand here?"

"I'm sorry," I replied, realizing my stupidity. "Come on in. Let me take your coat." I could not believe how gorgeous she was.

"Is something the matter?" she asked.

"No. Why?" I replied.

"You keep staring at me," she stated.

"It's just that ..." I fumbled for words. "You are *so* beautiful."

"You'd better quit talking like that," she told me.

"Why?"

"Because you are going to give me a swelled head," she responded, smiling. "I may start to like hearing it."

"Someone must have told you that by now," I said, lighting her cigarette and mine. "You must have heard it a thousand times."

She looked at the television, a large grin taking over her face. "No. I am not used to hearing it."

"I can't believe that," I replied. "I'm sure the doctors are always trying to take you home."

"Nope. Most of them are married."

"What about the unmarried ones?" I asked.

"Most of them are jerks, on a big ego trip," she replied. "They might proposition me once before I set them straight." She looked at me. "I'm very particular."

"Well, I feel honored," I told her, grinning.

"I'm beginning to think that you like me," she said.

"So am I," I softly admitted. "Let's get going to dinner."

"That sounds good."

"What did you tell Janet about me?" I asked her later at dinner.

"About what?" Pam responded.

"About what I am doing in Houston," I said.

"I told her that you had taken a vacation and are back looking for a job," she stated.

"That's good," I told her. "I don't want her to worry about you." I took a sip of my drink.

The restaurant Pam selected was very popular and was packed. So we waited by first having a drink at the bar. Backgammon games were going on around us, the competitors losing themselves in the alcohol, cigarettes, and contests. It was always interesting to watch people compete, because they are most themselves when the die are rolled, the cards dealt, or the starting gun fired. The combatants preserved well-mannered play, reaching game-deciding moves with fencers' aplomb … and, of course, the luck of the rolls. Skill seemed not so much in successful rolls but in making the best of opportunities occurring by chance.

"Do you play backgammon?" Pam asked, noticing my interest in the games around us.

"A little," I replied. "It has been a while since I last played."

"I have a set at home," she told me. "I hereby challenge you, Mr. Crabtree, to a winner-take-all series: five games." She raised her glass, a coy smile on her lips, and a mischievous look in her eyes.

"What are the stakes?" I questioned, raising my glass to meet hers.

"Time will tell, won't it?" she replied with a subtle grin.

"I hope so," I said.

What was I doing? I knew I was infatuated with Pam's grace, beauty, and charm, yet a portion of me was thinking about Karen. Pam was so warm, so unthreatening. I wanted to grab her, kiss her. Why?

Was it the need for companionship? Would anyone fill that need right now? Or was it Pam? She was sweet, unpretentious, and charming, seeming to enjoy my company, not intending any malevolence. She was intelligent, witty, and exceedingly beautiful. I was clownish, fighting undirected gales from deep within myself.

Pam caught me entranced but was not annoyed. "What's on your mind? You were staring a hole in the counter," she said.

"I was ..." I said, stammering in surprise, "just trying to make sense of all this."

"Sense of what?" she inquired, her attentive concern apparent. The slight tilt of her head was enamoring and disarming, my fears diffusing.

"You are truly beautiful," I absently uttered.

Pam grinned, scarlet blooming from her shoulders up. "What does that have to do with 'making sense of all this'?" she replied, taking another sip.

"I can't believe this," I began. "I'm arrested in my parents' home for an armed robbery, forced to fly back to Houston, and ..." I paused. "I run into one of the most beautiful women I have ever seen."

She did not visibly acknowledge my statement.

"What amazes me is that she seems to trust me—for God knows what reason—and enjoys my company," I told her. I paused, exchanging smiles with her. "Tell me," I started to inquire, "is it my money or my violin playing that keeps you here?"

She looked at me with mild surprise. "You play the violin?" she asked.

"No," I said. "I'm not rich, either, so it can't be those reasons."

Pam burst out laughing, setting her gaze into my eyes, shaking her head. "I don't know how you do it."

"Do what?"

"Here you are, facing an uncertain future, and yet you keep a sense of humor." She took a quick nip from her drink, her eyes briefly alleviating my anxiety, but only briefly. "How?"

I looked at the counter for a moment, afraid of the truth. Then I looked back at her. "I have to," I quietly confessed, "or I'll start screaming." I looked at her, at my glass. I took a gulp, warmth coating my throat. "I *must* laugh." My loquaciousness fled, smitten by the realization of its purpose. I had to laugh, had to smile, had to talk, to keep my mind off of my situation.

I caught Pam's expression, no longer jovial. She had not meant to probe so deeply and was openly apologetic.

"I did not mean to ..."

"That's all right," I said, cutting her short. "I have had time to study my thoughts and responses. We all need a defense mechanism occasionally."

Her head was slightly lowered, heavy with accidental insight.

"Besides," I began, grasping her hand. She looked up, seeming embarrassed. "I enjoy your company tremendously, which is worth a permanent smile."

"Thank you," she said, leaning toward me. I kissed her on the lips, softly, slowly. She leaned back. "I like you a lot. You're special," she said.

"I'll bet you say that to all the guys," I jested, squeezing her fingertips.

"You're right," she replied with a smile, the twinkle returning to her green eyes. She paused. "I hope it all turns out okay," she softly added.

"That makes at least two of us," I said.

"Aren't you *nervous*," she inquired, "not knowing how Monday's meeting will go?"

"What good would it do?" I answered, smiling a fake smile before becoming somber. "Yes, I am."

There was the momentary silence of an undesired admission. She looked away.

"I would rather not bother you with it this evening, Pam," I told her. "I would like to be half-decent company. I want you to have fun, not be afraid or upset."

"I *am* having a good time," she replied, taking my hand in both of hers.

"Thank you," I said and, leaning forward, kissed her more softly than before.

The bartender served us another round, but before we could take a sip we were called for seating. This restaurant offered all of the frills: the wine bottle cork ceremony, a centerpiece with two candles, and an expediter whose sole responsibility was our table. The food was excellent. We had a wonderful meal.

"Pam," I said between bites, "what would you like to do after dinner? This is your evening." I bit into a forkful of quiche.

"I thought we might go to my apartment," she replied. "Janet is supposed to bring her date there for a while. I want you to meet her."

"Very well," I replied.

"Is that okay?" she asked.

"Yes, its fine," I answered. "I have wanted to meet Janet anyway. She sounds very interesting."

"She is. You'll like her a lot. She's a doll," Pam said.

Pam was finished and I was nearly so when the barmaid approached our table. "Would you care for another drink?" she asked me.

"Pam?" I asked.

"No, thanks, Mike, this is enough," she replied.

"I agree." Turning to the barmaid, I told her, "Thank you, but we're doing fine." I looked over at Pam.

"I'm glad I met you," Pam softly spoke.

"Don't say that!" I retorted.

"Why not?" she asked, surprised, caught completely off-guard by my reply.

"You've not known me long enough."

"I don't think time will change my mind."

"You don't, huh?"

"No, I don't," she stated, stretching out her palm to me.

"I hope not," I told her, placing my hand in hers. "Are you ready to leave?"

"Whenever you are."

"Great! Let's go," I stated. "I can't *wait* to get back to your apartment," I hinted.

"Uh huh?" she grinned. "You have yet to beat me in backgammon," she said with a wink.

"I'm a fast learner," I told her.

"I'll bet you are," she replied, broadly smiling.

"Shall we?"

"Let's."

I paid the bill and we were off, into the evening. Houston had always seemed ambiguous to me, in that the white collars and blue collars jammed the highways to and from work, yet there was an emptiness permeating the glitter, tinsel of a city bursting at the seams. It was so huge and yet so hollow, volume without substance. Houston was the epitome of the boom town: lots of people and money but little integrity. Perhaps that was what most impressed me about Pam. She was neither theatrical nor timid, playing in a town of transience and mass anonymity. One could have the best or loneliest of times in Houston.

Tom and Janet entered after Pam and I arrived. They did not stay long. Pam and I settled comfortably on the couch. She was into music by Carole King, Leon Redbone, and Fleetwood Mac, as well as Broadway musicals and some light opera. The atmosphere was quiet and cozy, and we sat for the longest time just listening to music and talking. The funny part about it was that I was in no hurry to be aggressive. If and when this armed robbery mess was over, I would be able to see her again. It was late when she dropped me off at the hotel, after our quiet evening.

"Hello." My brother answered the telephone.

"Hello, Bobby?" I replied.

"Yeah," he said.

"Is Dad there? He wanted me to call him, to talk about what Mr. Paris had to say," I told him.

"He's in the other room," he replied. "I'll get him."

It was 11:00 AM in Houston. The family would be back from church. I knew they would not go anywhere today, at least not until after the football games. It would not have surprised me had three or four "adopted children" dropped by to watch the tube and eat popcorn. Sunday football games were an institution at the Crabtree house. My mother had become a pro at coordinating halftime and meal time, because she enjoyed the games as much as the other family members.

"Hello," Dad said.

"Dad?" I responded.

"What's up?" he asked.

"I'm getting nervous."

"That's to be expected," he replied. "We're nervous for you.

"I guess it's taken this long for everything to sink in."

"All you can do is follow Mr. Paris's instructions," he advised.

"Steve... uh, Mr. Paris will be ready to leave at one o'clock," I said. "If I could only find out the date.... That's all I need."

"You'll get that tomorrow," Dad replied. "Then it'll just be a matter of time before you're clear."

"I'll tell you what; for their sakes, I almost hope that they have concrete evidence against me!" I said loudly. "I'm tired of being jacked around. I'll sue the hell out of them if this is unnecessary!"

"It's too early to talk about suing," he calmly replied.

"I know, Dad," I dejectedly said, my summed boldness becoming so much air. "I just feel so *helpless.*"

"Things will change, one way or the other, tomorrow," he stated.

There was a momentary stillness, awkward yet necessary. The truth was to be had, but tomorrow ... tomorrow—immediate and distant, pass or fail.

"Mike," Dad said.

"Yeah, Dad?"

"Take it easy, tonight. Just relax."

"Okay, Dad."

"I'll talk to you after you get back from Columbus," he told me, as instruction.

"Dad ..." I began.

"Yeah."

"Thanks."

"Yeah," he replied after noticeable hesitation.

"Bye," I told him.

The street was fairly empty. There were a few pedestrians killing time, window shopping without the ability to buy. I imagined half of them dreamers, the other half realists: the former wishing they could, the latter knowing they could not. I opened a beer. This room, so empty, was beginning to seem like a cage. I had friends in town but was not allowed to see them.

"Here I am," I said to my reflection in the mirror. "What the hell? Why me?" I took a gulp. It was warm, the beers having been bought yesterday and left in a bag by the sink. "What did I do to deserve this?" I yelled at the ceiling. "What good does yelling do, Mike?" I asked my reflection. "No one wants to hear about it." I decided to go for a walk.

The air was brilliant, sharp, like an animated excitement. The Texas sun, peeking now and then from between buildings caused me to warm, then chill, then warm. Light became shadow, freedom became submission. They, around me in their own worlds of living, did not notice. These buildings, so tall; the high clouds seemed immune to man's frustrations, his vanity. A wino had passed out in the alley and did not seem to care. He laughed and cried his own destiny. The air around me seemed less excited. Or maybe it was just me.

"Mike," I said myself: "What are you doing? What about Karen? Shouldn't you call her?"

"Oh, excuse me!" I told the man with whom I had collided, not paying attention to where I was going.

"Are you using Pam?"

"I don't think so."

"Why not?"

"I genuinely care for her."

"Have you ever cared enough to not be protective or elusive?"

I could not answer that question. It hurt. I thought about Anna, then Karen. Then I refused to think about it. The mind can be redirected, I learned from necessity. The most difficult task was discovering or creating a pleasant perspective, or remembering how it seemed when it last felt pleasant. It was easy to become lost in one's own mind, having closed all of the entrances to anything or anyone else.

Returning to the hotel, I decided to call Karen. She would be able to give me support. She always had. I dialed the front desk but hung up. Sooner or later I had to support myself. If I was using anyone, it was Karen, and she was making it too easy for me to do so. I settled on the bed and watched the football game.

Pam dropped by around dusk. She was stunning. Her hair flowed over her head like silk, dashing over her shoulders. The green eyes had been surrounded by just enough makeup. Her cheeks were red from the cold.

"Come in. Come in, please," I told her.

"Thank you," she said.

I opened the door and grasped her coat. "It must have gotten colder since I went out."

"It has," she replied: "Windy, too."

"Please, have a seat," I offered, pulling one from beneath the circular table in the corner. "What did you have planned tonight?"

"Nothing definite," she replied.

"Me neither," I said, thinking that I wanted to kiss her.

"I know of a little club you would enjoy," she began. "They changed an old gas station into a nightclub. The interior is really well done."

She was right. I had a great time. We parked in front of the hotel after returning. "Thank you," I told her. "I had a wonderful time."

"I'm supposed to say that," she stated. "You stole my line," she snapped, half-giggling beneath her pretended sulk.

"So sue me," I replied, laughing. "Anyway, you'll have to wait your turn."

Her look became stern, as though I had said something wrong.

"I'm sorry, Pam," I said apologetically. "I didn't mean that." It was more hurt than stern. I paused. "I had better let you get back to your apartment. I've had you out late these last few nights. You probably could use some sleep." Still no change in the look on her face. I opened the car door and stepped out.

"Mike," Pam said.

"Yes, Pam?" I replied, sticking my head back into the car.

"Call me tomorrow evening. Will you?" she asked, reaching for my hand.

"I will. I promise."

She leaned toward me. We kissed, though not at all softly. I closed the door and she pulled away. I was wishing I had tried to stop her, even if for a short while.

The wakeup call came at 9:00 AM. By 10 I was ready to go. I called Mr. Paris's office. Sharon told me Mr. Paris wanted me to bring my luggage in case the police wanted me to stay in or near Columbus. The schedule had not changed: one o'clock.

A coffee shop one block down Texas Avenue served very good hash brown potatoes. I sat at the counter, drinking coffee, looking at the people around me. They were all here for the same purpose: to make a living. For so many, Houston was a phase through which people passed, an economic stepping stone for something more genuinely desired.

Noon surprised me, having crept up on me while I was deep in thought. Time was determined to carry me with it. There was no nervousness, ominous anxiety having dissipated. I had worried and feared enough. I was not able to turn back, so why fight it? I knew I was innocent. This would be the start of proving it.

I felt odd, dropping my suitcase in the foyer in front of Mr. Paris's office. The stares did not really bother me as I had walked down the sidewalk, suitcase in hand, and into the building. It was more the feeling of being a vagabond that penetrated my senses.

Mr. Paris was still at lunch when I arrived a few minutes early. When he walked in, he was impressive. He was splendidly attired in a dark gray, European-cut vested suit with black pinstripes. He looked like a distinguished-clothing advertisement in a businessmen's periodical. I could just imagine the looks on the faces of the Colorado County police when this nobody from Virginia walks in with his double-barrel lawyer cocked and ready to shoot.

"Hi, Mike. Are you ready to go?" he asked on his way to his office.

"Any time you are, Steve," I replied, dropping the magazine I had been scanning.

"I'll get the car and meet you in front of the building," he told me. He pocketed some petty cash that Sharon gave him and then said, "Let's be off."

I was not surprised by his taste in cars. The silver Continental, its wax job shining, pulled to the curb. The trunk popped open, and I placed my bags inside. I was surprised, however, when I sat down in the front passenger seat. Steve had tuned the radio to one of Houston's rock-and-roll FM stations.

"Nice car you have," I told Steve.

"It's comfortable and dependable," he said. "One of the job's benefits."

"Benefits?" I asked.

"Yes," he replied. "It is a tax write-off."

"That's convenient," I stated. I looked over the gray leather interior. The music was a puzzle to me. "If you have that station on for me, you can change it," I told him. "I like all kinds of music."

"I like this station, too," he replied. He glanced at me and laughed. "What? Do I look over-the-hill or something?"

"I didn't mean it that way," I responded. "I just thought that your taste in music might be more like—"

"Symphonies?" Steve said, cutting me off.

"Yeah, or easy-listening, like James Taylor, the Carpenters, or B.J. Thomas," I told him.

"Why?" he asked. "Because I'm a lawyer and more 'sophisticated'?"

"Something like that," I replied.

"That's a bunch of crap," he stated. "I'm just like anyone else."

I had not considered that point. There was a social mystique about professionals such as doctors or lawyers, although Steve made it seem unwarranted. Most people held those in esteem whom they considered to be of social prominence, sort of building pedestals out of their own perspectives.

"Does that 'sophisticated' stuff bother you?" I asked.

"Not too much," he replied. "It gets in the way occasionally."

Steve was very knowledgeable and witty, an interesting person to talk with. The conversation dispelled my anxiousness and seemed to quicken the trip. We discussed the case and the police's handling of it.

He told one story I laughed at for probably ten minutes.

"Have you ever been arrested, Steve?" I asked.

"No. I was stopped once, by two policemen I knew," he stated.

"What happened?"

"I had been at a Texas Bar Association picnic in Austin," he began. He looked over at me with a grin. "It was real hot and becoming humid. I drank a beer—one beer—and it really seemed to affect me. I guess it was the heat."

"Yeah?" I uttered.

"Well, I got into the car and began driving," he continued. "The effect of the beer must have been reflected in my driving, because the policemen pulled me over."

"What did they say when they saw it was you?"

"They laughed," he said, "and then asked me if I was sober."

"What'd you do?"

"I told them that I was," Steve answered, "and could prove it." He paused.

"And ...?"

"They told me to prove it, then laughed," he said. We both chuckled.

"How did you prove it?" I asked.

"I asked them if they would let me go if I did a back flip off the car's trunk," he replied.

I burst out laughing. I could envision the entire scene. "Did you make it?"

"No," he answered. "I busted my ass."

We were both laughing.

"But they told me it was close enough," he said, looking into my face.

I was laughing hard.

"They said, 'work on it,' and they let me go."

"That's funny!" I told him between laughs.

"They thought so," he replied.

Heading west from Houston on Interstate 10, the scenery was rather plain until Eagle Lake, where the flatland became hilly. The grass and brush became trees. The scenery distracted me. It was not until the Columbus exit was in sight that my nervousness returned.

"Here we are, Mike," Steve said. He noticed the concern on my face. "Don't worry," he told me. "If you are innocent, we will be able to prove it."

"I am innocent," I told him.

This road, which I had frequently traveled, seemed to be waiting for me. We pulled to the curb in front of the white county jailhouse.

Steve looked at me and then checked the contents of his briefcase. "You let me do the talking, except for answering questions. Got that?" he instructed.

"Yes," I replied.

"Well, let's go to it!" he stated.

Ironically, my steps were assured and purposive. This was it; I was ready. Steve stepped up to the oak door and entered. He waited for me to join him, which took a resolved moment.

"Hello," he said to an elderly clerk behind a tall, black counter. "I am Steve Paris."

"Mr. Paris," the officer began. "Oh, yes. You're representing Crabtree?"

"That's correct," he stated. "I am here to see Captain Brooks."

"You are to meet him at the Weimar City Hall building," he said. He looked at me. "Is this Crabtree?"

His eyes were a sharp blue, sunken with age. His cheeks were high, long, and narrow, culminating in a pointed chin. The hairline had beaten a path up, over his scalp, leaving him with two sparse patches of silver hair. He could be a very stern man, judging from his general appearance.

Steve did not answer the man's question. "How do you get to Weimar?" Steve asked, breaking the clerk's stare at me.

"Get back on Alternate 90 here, behind the station," he began, gesturing and pointing as he spoke. "Head on west through the town. It's seventeen miles. The City Hall is on the left side, just after the railroad tracks. Go in the entrance furthest to the left. That's Chief Teoson's office. He'll be there."

"Would you call him," Steve requested, "to let him know we are on our way?"

"Right away," he replied.

"Thank you," Steve said.

"Yep," replied the clerk.

I turned and preceded Steve to the car. "Well, another delay," I said to Steve as he closed his door.

"This is a very ill-managed case; I will admit that," Steve stated.

"I still believe that I have never been to Weimar," I informed Steve. "I'll know as soon as we get there." A few moments later, I asked, "They will have to tell me the date of the crime when they officially charge me, won't they?"

"Yes," Steve answered.

"Good," I replied. "That's all I need."

"Are you sure, Mike?" Steve asked.

"Positive," I emphatically stated. "Please make a point to get to the crime's date as soon as possible."

"We'll see how it goes," he stated.

"All right," I said. I was silent the rest of the way to Weimar.

I had never been there. We came upon the city limit sign on Alternate 90. There was nothing familiar about the town. The municipal building was ahead, past the tracks, on the left. It was a single story tall, made of gray brick, with three doors and a large picture window on the front side. I told Steve I had never been here. We approached the new building with steady steps. I opened the door and waited for Steve to pass me.

Steve spoke with poise, resonant and well enunciated. "Hello, I am Steve Paris," he stated. "I have brought my client, Mr. Crabtree, in for questioning."

A large, red-haired man with graying temples and a mustache stepped from behind a desk on the right side of the room. "I am Chief Teoson," he boomed. "This," he said, gesturing toward a man behind a second desk, in the room's center, "is Captain Brooks."

So that is Brooks, I thought, almost aloud.

Steve stepped toward each, shaking each man's hand, and then motioned me toward the desk behind which Brooks was standing. Brooks was wearing a white shirt and a small, dark tie. He had oily jet-black hair and a small mustache. The hair was combed from the face back, tapered to the base of his neck. He was about my height and weight but with a bit of a paunch.

"This," Steve told the men, "is Mr. Crabtree." I shook hands with the two officers and then sat in one of two chairs in front of the center desk. The brown tile floor reflected the blandness of the tan walls. A policeman walked through a back door, handed Teoson a form, and left.

Teoson stated, "We need to take a set of prints and a few pictures, for identification purposes. Have you altered your appearance in any manner while in Virginia?"

"Yes," I told them with a little unease, "I have. I had a beard, which I shaved off."

"That is too bad," Brooks said, playing with a pencil. "It will make identification more difficult." He remained somewhat animated to this point, scrutinizing my movements and response.

"Stand up and we'll get a front view and profile shot," Teoson instructed me.

Holding a placard in front of me, with numbers and a date, I was nervous as the pictures were taken. Those done, Teoson had said that fingerprints were also necessary. He opened a portable fingerprinting kit, placing it on a counter behind his desk. The instruction to join him was a nod and "Mr. Crabtree."

My mind stepped momentarily into the experience in Virginia Beach. This would be just another replay. It was. Dab in ink and roll from left to right. It was quickly done, and I washed my hands before returning to my seat.

Steve spoke up when I was seated. "Gentlemen, my client wants to know what he is being charged with."

"Before we read the charges against you," Teoson began, "have you been read your rights?"

"Yes, I have," I replied.

"Just the same," he stated, "I will read them to you again, in the presence of your attorney."

"Thank you," Steve said, nodding to the chief.

The air was thick with legality. It had been nine days since my arrest. I was thinking quickly yet was aware of Brooks's scrutiny, Chief Teoson's words, the brown floor, the ticking clock on the far wall, and Steve's practiced focus. The sunlight coming through the window was a brightening presence spreading across the otherwise bland floor.

This was yesterday's "tomorrow." The replays were finished. It was finally here, pass or fail. My teeth ground.

"You understand these rights as I have read them to you?" Teoson concluded.

"Yes, I do," I replied.

Brooks began, "Michael Wayne Crabtree, you are hereby accused by the County of Colorado, the State of Texas, under the statutes of the United States of America ..."

Finally, the Truth

A few rings preceded her voice. "Hello?" Barbara answered the telephone.

"Barb, it's Mike," I replied, trying to suppress my emotions.

"Mom! Dad!" I heard her loudly say. "It's Mike!"

She could not wait for what the meeting had produced. "What'd they say?" she excitedly inquired. Before I could speak I heard another receiver being picked up.

"Hi, hon." It was Mom.

"Hello," I said, trying to remain calm.

"Wait a moment," Mom said, "until your father gets on the other line."

"Aw, *shucks!*" Barbara exclaimed, handing the telephone to my father.

"Hello," Dad said.

"Hi, Dad," I replied.

"Well," my mother anxiously began: "What happened?"

"I met with the police in Weimar, not Columbus," I began.

"And ...?" she questioned. I emotionally recounted to them the story.

"At 8:55 PM, on the twelfth of December, nineteen hundred seventy-eight," Brooks read monotonically.

My face lit up like an explosion; I was overjoyed and furious! "That's it!" I whispered to Steve. I was innocent and could absolutely prove it. It was my chance to show them. "I can prove that I was not

143

in the state that evening," I stated aloud, staring at Brooks. *What a waste of time and money!* I thought. I was angry.

"How is that?" Brooks replied.

I looked at Steve for permission to proceed. He nodded.

"I left Houston at 5:30 AM on the morning of the twelfth," I answered, meekly at first, but with snowballing conviction. "I have a witness to that fact."

Brooks questioned: "Who is that?"

"Gary Weekley, in Houston," I replied.

"Oh, *geez*," Brooks unexpectedly uttered, looking at the ceiling as though for help.

"You have heard of him?" Steve quickly responded, ready to take a note.

"Let's just say that he's come up in this case," Brooks said.

"There's *more!*" I stated, not wanting to put up with any further delay.

"What's that?" Teoson spoke.

"I stayed at a hotel in Alabama that evening," I began. *"In fact,"* I emphasized, "I made a collect telephone call from the hotel to my parents, in Virginia, at about 6:30 PM, to inform them that I was on my way to Virginia." I continued, gaining momentum. "It could *not* have been my truck, because I drove it, full of my belongings!" I stared into Brooks' face, furious. "I registered the truck at the hotel when I checked in," I stated, my voice emphatic and angrily tense.

Brooks and Teoson took notes. Steve had not lost a word of my explanation. My pulse was racing with anger and elation. Essentially, upon being read the charges, it was over.

The rest of the session was mere formality. I did not try to implicate Kevin because it occurred to me that he may have been as much a pawn in their games as I had. It had all come down to the crime's date, to which Brooks had willfully and intentionally denied me knowledge. All of the worry, time, and expense could have been eliminated if Brooks had told my father on December 30—the date of my arrest—that the crime had occurred on the evening of the twelfth.

"That's it, Dad," I told him, completing my recap of the meeting. Dad was silent.

"That's *great*, hon!" Mom said.

"I'm glad it is over," I softly stated.

"So am I," she replied.

"I have to call Steve Paris tomorrow," I told them, "to find out when they will allow me to come home."

Dad was silent.

"Come home as soon as possible," Mom said.

"Brooks," my father began, noticeably upset, "told you the date was the *twelfth*?" he asked, with incredulity.

"Yes, sir," I told him, already having felt the anger that I knew he must be feeling.

"When you were arrested," Dad responded, "I told him you left Texas that day."

"I know, Dad," I replied.

"He told me it had occurred about a week before that day!" Dad stated, his anger swelling.

"I know, Dad. I already remembered all that," I said.

Dad again became silent. I began talking about the need to prove my alibi, getting hold of telephone records, and locating that small hotel in Alabama. Mom had said she would get busy on that. Then I was finished.

"Call us Thursday, and let us know what is going on," Mom said, breaking the long-distance static.

"Will do," I replied. "Mom," I said, my voice starting to crack.

"Yes, Mike?" she said.

"Thank you ... and Dad, you, too," I said, or tried to say, as I was crying with tears of relief and thankfulness. Praise God for these two. They did not want to doubt me, even when I was questioning myself as far as being an unwitting and unknowing participant. My parents' unresolved doubt was a tension between what they believed they had instilled in me and what the objective evidence would demonstrate. How could they have an unquestioning faith in me when the police's

145

purported facts could prove my vehicle's presence if not also mine? All could only wait for the facts.

Between sniffles, Mom uttered: "Yeah, hon."

"Mike …" Dad began but could not finish.

"I'll call you on Thursday," I told them, ending the conversation. "Bye, Mom and Dad," I said, and hung up. I lay down on the bed of my new hotel room, on the west side of Houston, nearer Columbus, and cried out my pent-up emotions for twenty minutes.

The receipt from my stay in the Alabama hotel had been thrown away, so the proof of my whereabouts on the evening of the twelfth would be found in the telephone company records. Mom had said she would check into it immediately.

I could not, for the life of me, remember the name of the little Alabama town, north of Mobile, in which I had stayed. The police would not allow me to go until I had conclusively validated my story. It angered me that they could hold me without validating theirs.

Pam was excited by my new information, as I spewed it to her over the phone. There was no longer the necessity for a sounding board, so the potential relationship between us gained dimensionally. She had been a friend in my need. Now, the friendship could be broadened and deepened.

"What about Karen?" I asked myself, having completed the conversation with Pam. "If you stop seeing Pam …" No. I did not want that. "Karen has been waiting. She is waiting for you now. What do you want from her? What do you want *for* her?" Still no answers.

Indecision is the inability to step with both feet simultaneously in different directions. Such an attempt leaves you flat on your back. The non-attempt leaves you in a perpetual spot: indecision having impeded transition, essentially paralyzing activity. It is a senseless paralysis, in that the ability to act is not taken away, but surrendered to that which exists only as mental possibilities. Which direction? The next step must be made with both feet, for all that exists is what the mind makes of it, and others are free to make their own decisions.

I decided to visit my friends in the apartment complex where I had been living. Bus routes ran by the hotel two blocks away, so the first thing in the morning, I would depart. Little did I know that the next day's events would drastically alter my understanding of the entire case.

The morning traffic on Interstate 10 was horrendous: cars inching like a tremendous centipede, each motion chased by the unit behind the mover. People chose this unnerving chase. Horns honked. People cursed. All the while, clouds rained upon the asphalt.

The air was damp and cold, my coat offering its appreciated protection but without complete success. Humid, windy cold was the most miserable of weather. Each step toward the bus stop was more difficult than the previous, as I second-guessed my decision to leave so early in the day. I was glad that the sky cleared some during the bus trip; I had to walk the last mile to the apartment complex.

Most of my ex-neighbors had gone to work. Susan, the wife of a friend on the upper floor, was home. She was slow, as usual, in responding to the knocks on the front door.

"Yeah?" I heard her through the door. "Who is it?"

"Susan, it's Mike ... Crabtree," I told her.

"Oh!" she exclaimed. She undid the chain and unlocked the door. We embraced in a quick hug.

"Hi!" I said. "How have you been?"

"Not much new," she replied. She walked to the table near the kitchen. "Vernon and I are getting a divorce," she said.

"I'm sorry to hear that," I told her.

"Well," she replied, "it just didn't work out."

I was genuinely sorry to hear the news. Susan and Vernon were young and caught up in their romance: Susan, only eighteen, especially. Her parents didn't approve of him, or of her getting married. Their wedding ceremony was brief and nice, held beside the pool at the apartments and presided over by a justice of the peace. They had little money. There were few decorations, no elaborate gowns or flowers. Since her parents did not approve of the wedding, and did not attend, Susan asked me to give away the bride. I was honored as their friend. All of our neighbors watched the ceremony from their apartment balconies and doorsteps. Everyone applauded when the groom kissed his bride. The reception was a pool party, lasting well into the night.

"Have you gotten that mess straightened out with the police?" she asked. "They were all over this complex, asking for you," she told me, her slender head tilting slightly on its fragile neck, her straight, shoulder-length light brown hair not yet brushed.

"It's almost over," I replied. "I'm back here to straighten things out."

"What was the problem?" she inquired.

"A county about seventy miles from here wanted me for an armed robbery," I explained.

"You know they arrested Kevin, don't you?" she added.

"Yes," I replied. "He is probably as innocent as I am."

"He is out on bail right now," she said. "He might be home."

"What apartment is he in?" I asked.

"Thirty-three," she replied.

"I think I'll drop by and see him, after a while," I told her. "He must have a story to tell, himself."

I was about to begin concluding our conversation several minutes later when there was a knock on her door. Susan opened the door.

There stood Kevin Silver. "Would you mind . . . ?" Kevin began, but stopped upon seeing me. "Hey! Mike!" he exclaimed. "I thought you were in jail." He was perhaps six years older than me, a few inches taller. His face was oval, and he was rapidly balding, his reddish patches of hair growing smaller with time.

"I was for three days," I stated. "I waived extradition in Virginia and came back to straighten this thing out." I lit a cigarette. Susan remained standing by the door, holding the knob, astonished.

"*Damn!*" she exclaimed, looking at me. She could not imagine me in jail.

"For sure!" Kevin replied as he came through the door. "The story of your arrest was in the Weimar paper, on the front page." Susan's face was still covered with astonishment, her mouth open.

"I'll have to read it," I said. "I was told of your arrest." I paused, taking a puff of the cigarette. "What all happened?"

"This whole thing has been *crazy!*" Kevin stated. "The police came to the rig on the thirteenth, asking a bunch of stuff about the truck and your whereabouts. I told them that you had left to return to Virginia." The three of us sat down at the table.

Kevin continued. "Then they told me not to leave the rig for a while."

"Didn't they tell you what was going on?" Susan inquired.

"Not at the time," he replied. "They returned later and arrested me on the fourteenth."

"You were arrested on the fourteenth?" I asked.

"Yeah," he stated. "They held me for six days in that old county jailhouse."

"How did you get out?" I inquired.

"The sixth day," he explained, "they finally allowed me to call a lawyer. I contacted the ACLU and was out on bail that afternoon."

"Geez," I said.

"That sounds rough," Susan stated.

"It was," Kevin replied. "The food was terrible."

"I'll agree there," I told them.

"They questioned me twice," Kevin continued, "without a lawyer, and put me through two line-ups."

"That's illegal!" I responded, anger compounding.

"The lawyer said that too," Kevin replied, shaking his head. "The most incredible thing was what happened one morning ..."

"How's that?" I interjected.

"They put me in a line-up, and the eyewitness could not make up her mind.... It was the first time," he explained.

"And ...?" I coaxed.

"They brought me into the lobby and had me sit down. In walks this woman I've never seen before," he stated, becoming animated.

"Later, she picks me out of a line-up, but when she walked in we exchanged a pleasant 'good morning.'"

"You mean ..." Susan piped up, "she didn't recognize you until after seeing you in the jail?"

"That's right," Kevin stated.

"They did you wrong, Kevin," I told him.

"Sure as hell," he replied.

Susan got some beers from the kitchen. As she returned from the refrigerator, there was another knock on the door. "Again ...?" she responded. "Who can it be now?" She dropped the beers off on the table and went to the door, opening it.

Bryan looked at Susan. "Susan," he asked, "have you seen Kevin?" He stood in the door, in blue jeans, hiking boots, and a blue, fleece-lined vest over a flannel shirt. As usual for him, he stood with his fingertips inside the tops of his pants' front pockets.

She glanced over her shoulder at us. "Yeah," she told him.

Bryan followed the line of her glance and bolted in. "Mike!" he loudly stated, reaching out his hand. "*What the hell*, man?!" He grabbed my hand, shaking it vigorously. "I thought you'd be in jail!"

"I was," I replied, our hands separating. "I had to come back and turn myself in."

Over the next ten minutes, I told them my story of the previous nine days. Susan's head did not stop shaking with astonishment. Kevin simply nodded at those parts coinciding with his own experience.

"Then," Bryan asked: "it *wasn't* your truck?"

He had placed his forearms on the table and was leaned toward me. His long, curly brown hair swayed as he shook his head. Bryan was twenty-three, like me. His face was narrow, with a small nose and a long forehead. He had bright blue eyes. The lips were thin, and he had a dimple. Bryan was smaller than me, at about five foot eight. His frame had put on muscle over the year, but he was already firm from his years of working on his parents' potato farm in Maine.

"No," I answered. "My truck was with me in Alabama."

Kevin stated, "They told me they had an open-and-shut case on you!"

"Me, too!" Bryan said. "They told me they could prove Kevin guilty, too."

"That's what they told me about you, Kevin," I said. "It seems we've all been had."

"I'll say," Kevin angrily spat.

We spent most of the day exchanging accounts of the events. Bryan had been in Mexico and Kevin had been in Houston when the crime occurred. Both had reliable witnesses to uphold their alibis.

I came to understand that the police, Captain Brooks as well, had nothing on any of us. It had been a witch-hunt, trying to solve a crime. I did not know how they came up with my license plate number as evidence. Somebody made a stupid error in judgment and then perpetrated an unlawful sequence of events in abusing police authority to detain and apprehend citizens. The authority entrusted to the police by us citizens had been absurdly abused.

"I wonder how many people doing time were railroaded as they tried to do to us," I stated. "If I had not checked into that hotel or called my parents, how the hell could I have proven I was not involved?" I blew another cloud of cigarette smoke. "If I had simply pulled into a rest area to nap, instead of getting a room, how could I prove where I was?"

Bryan shook his head. Kevin looked at the floor, perhaps not previously considering the frightening implications of five years or more in jail, just because *someone* was going to be found guilty of a crime. Susan sat stupefied.

"Everyone at the rig has been concerned," Bryan stated. "They'd like to see you. I go back to work tomorrow night. Why don't you go with me?"

"I'll have to check it out with my lawyer," I told Bryan. "I'm supposed to call him this afternoon to find out when I might be able to go home."

"Go ahead and call him," Bryan insisted. He was always frank and direct, a reflection of his Maine upbringing. I did as he wanted.

"Evans and Paris, may I help you."

"David?" I asked.

"Yes?" he replied.

"This is Mike Crabtree."

"Hello, Mike," he said. "What can I do for you?"

"I was wondering if my bond allowed me to leave the county," I told him.

"Yes, it does," he answered.

I told David, "I was supposed to call Steve this afternoon, about my return to Virginia."

David informed me, "He's not in at the moment, but he left a message for you to call him on Thursday."

"Will do," I replied. "Thank you."

"What's up?" Bryan asked as I hung up the telephone.

"I can go to the rig, if nothing comes up," I told him. "I have to call my attorney again on Thursday."

"Come on to the rig!" Bryan repeated, coaxing. "Where are you staying?"

"Over off I-10, in a hotel by Gessner," I replied.

"Would you mind if I stayed with you?" he asked. We could leave from there and go to Sealy."

"Sounds okay to me," I told him.

We eventually left Susan's apartment. Bryan and I walked toward his truck. Bryan was slightly bow-legged, and he walked with his hands tucked into his blue jeans. It made his shoulders sway as he walked. There in the bed of the truck was Bryan's companion, Sam.

"Hello, Sam," I loudly said to the black Labrador retriever as he stood on his hind legs, the front legs resting on the top of the truck bed, his tail wagging rapidly.

"It's okay, Sam," Bryan told him as we approached the truck, still more than twenty feet away. That was Bryan's permission for Sam to get out of the truck. Sam leaped out of the back and came running toward me. I stopped and crouched. Sam ran excitedly to me, pushing his muzzle into my hand, his tail wagging excitedly. He walked around me, in circles, as I petted him.

"*Good boy*, Sam," I said. "Have you missed me?" Sam stopped his circling, putting a foreleg into my hand. He raised his head and licked me. "I missed you, too, Sam," I said. I stood, resuming my walk to the truck. Sam was a very smart and friendly dog. Bryan had trained him to respond to verbal commands. I had been around Bryan and Sam since training as a roughneck, almost a year earlier. We had worked together the entire year, until I left for Virginia.

"Get in the truck," Bryan instructed Sam, opening the truck door. Sam took two steps toward the open door, and then came back a step toward me. "In the truck!" Bryan repeated. Sam did as he was told, and climbed into the cab. I walked around to the passenger door and got in. Sam sat in the middle of the bench seat, in his familiar spot whenever I was in the truck. He pushed his muzzle against the side of my face.

"Yes, Sam," I told him, raising my hand to pet him, "you're a good boy." He was happy.

After she had gotten home from work, I called Pam from the hotel, asking if I could drop by and introduce her to Bryan. She said sure, that she would be home that evening. I introduced Pam to Bryan. He was quite impressed with her but told me I was chasing a dream.

Perhaps he was right. He had seen me get wrapped up with two ladies that year, neither of which panned out, and both of which ended up with me feeling self-deceived. A goal was one thing: tangible, constructive. A dream could be quite another: imaginary, sometimes spastic, but frequently beautiful and almost real. It was sometimes difficult to distinguish the two, other than by measurement of progressive activity. I could not now figure with which woman I was living a dream: which relationship should have been a goal. They affected me differently, offering no basis for comparison.

Bryan was his brash, boisterous self, which Pam did not seem to like. It probably did not help either that Bryan brought Sam into her apartment without first obtaining permission. After a short stay, of which our collective welcome was not as long, we went back to the hotel. I had given Pam a quick kiss, telling her I would call, and advising her I was going to be away for many days, in Sealy. She said she would see me when I got back.

During the drive back to the hotel, Bryan voiced his opinion of the situation with Pam, not knowing anything at all about Karen back in Virginia. "Mike," he told me, "you are setting yourself up for another fall."

Bryan did not know the meaning of "tact," as it was not in his New England nature. He always spoke the truth as he saw it, and without hesitation. "Consider it from her standpoint," he said. "If you were her, young and beautiful, with guys wanting to be with you all of the time, would you be happy with a fellow who was only around a couple days each week? Staying at home, missing a social life?"

I did not really try to argue my side, as I did not know what that side might be. Instead, I mostly listened, hoping that Bryan could be wrong, but knowing he was most likely right. I thought back to the window shoppers I had seen from the downtown hotel.

Bryan and I went to a pool hall and shot several games. We drank some beer and talked, him catching me up on the rig's whereabouts and the goings-on of the crewmembers. Not much had changed in the month that I had been gone. We returned to the hotel and called it a night.

We left Houston the next day, just after dark, after rush-hour traffic had died down. The drive was uneventful, once past the small town of Katy. There was little development west of Gessner Road, with the exception of a new commercial complex named "Park Ten" that was being constructed way off by itself to the west of the city. The developers believed that Houston would continue to spread west and had put much money into that development. We passed Brookshire and then there was nothing but farmland and night's darkness all the way to Sealy.

The iron derrick of T.L. Drilling Company Rig #2 stood as a finger of light in the darkness of the Texan sky. The rig could be seen from twenty miles away because the land around Sealy was flat and the few trees not very tall. Steve Paris and I had passed the rig on the way to Columbus on Monday, and I pointed out the derrick to him at that time, not knowing from that distance that it was the rig on which I had been working.

The work involved in drilling a hole miles into the ground was strenuous, dangerous, and dirty. Roughnecks, often referred to as "oilfield trash" in southeast Texas, were a breed of people seldom seen elsewhere. They were migrant workers in the most genuine sense, working day and night, hundreds—sometimes thousands—of miles away from loved ones, in the most extreme weather conditions. Danger was a constant companion. Rigs had killed and crippled many a man over the years. Needing to trust each other with their lives and safety, roughnecks had the most enduring of friendships and heated of disagreements. And many had slowly destroyed themselves in reaction to the loneliness.

Billy Joe Fields was one such man. With the heart of a child and an inability to cope with his lonely life, he was slowly drinking and smoking himself to death. I had not met a more jovial and kind person than this "good ole" Louisiana country boy who never grew up. He was our crew's driller, running the machinery to drill the wells. While working for BJ, as everyone called him, my relationship with him had become more than boss and employee.

When I first started and didn't have any, BJ lent me money so I could eat. He bought me beer after work in many a little Texas roadside honky-tonk. He was genuinely a good friend and, regardless of his problems, a good-hearted person. BJ had seen more trouble from drinking and drunken fights in his forty-two years than any five other persons I knew, combined. Seeing him brought a huge smile to my face.

He was standing, as I had seen him countless times, in the back of the small metal building on the rig floor, fidgeting with a pencil. "What's up, BJ?" I asked, stepping into the "doghouse," as it was called.

"I'll be damned!" he hollered, like a ghost had come up and tapped him on the shoulder. We met in the center of the building, shaking hands as if to break loose each other's arm.

"W-w-when did you get out of jail?" he asked.

"I've been out about a week," I told him. "I had to come back here and face the police."

"How'd it go?" he asked.

I grinned and told him, "I can prove I'm innocent."

"That's good," he replied. "Everyone here knew you couldn't have done it," he stated, moving back toward his favorite position, where he was when I entered. "We were all wondering if you would come by the rig."

"I thought I'd drop by to let everyone know I was okay," I said.

"You've got a job here if you want one," BJ stated.

"Thanks, BJ," I replied.

Sam trotted through the door, followed by Bryan. "Ain't that some crap?!" Bryan exclaimed.

BJ looked at me. "You know you were front page news in the W-W-Weimar paper, don't you?" BJ said, stuttering.

"That's what Bryan was telling me," I replied.

"I have a copy in the truck, behind the seat," BJ stated. "I'll show it to you in the morning."

"I'd like to see it."

BJ began fidgeting with the pencil. He always seemed very nervous, stuttering and stammering due to a high-strung nature. We would often complete words and phrases when talking with him, at times, so flustered would he become at the inability to make his thoughts verbal. He did not mind our help because, after all, everyone desires to be understood. We would at times kid him about it, telling him to relax and slow down his speaking. It seemed to work ... for a while.

In the morning, BJ opened his truck and gave me the newspaper. The newspaper account was indeed interesting. I thought it an ambiguous statement of society that public media were capable of creating notoriety, of imputing without personal or individual responsibility, and often printing that which was solely the word of authority figures without having fully investigated the foundations or implications of assertion.

I thought back to the two Norfolk/Virginia Beach newspapers that did not publish news of my arrest. Had *they* made the decision to not publish news of my arrest, until the process of fact-finding was complete, and actual charges were handed down via an indictment? I did not know.

The description of the truck used in the crime was "dark blue," but mine was a faded sky blue. The article did not include that discrepancy, as they were probably not aware of the discrepancy. They published what they were told as fact.

"What are you going to do?" BJ asked.

I looked around at the early morning light refracting through dew clinging to grass of the field surrounding the rig. "I don't know, BJ," I replied. "Before this is all over, it will have cost me the money that I saved and took back to Virginia for college."

"Good grief!" BJ exclaimed.

"I know," I told him. "Unless I can win a lawsuit against the police, I'll never see that money again."

BJ put the newspaper behind his seat and then turned to me, his door still open. "Come on!" he said. "Let's go get a beer."

"Sounds good to me," I replied, walking around to the passenger side.

The trip to Eagle Lake was not very long with respect to mileage, but the change from flatland and open fields to the slight roll of the land and much larger trees was very noticeable. We went as usual, when in this general area, to a little bar off State Highway 102, about fourteen miles from Eagle Lake. The shack had probably only five hundred square feet of space. The owner, an old oilfield hand with an affinity for hunting, lived in a quaint little house in front of and slightly to the right of the bar, as one approached from the highway. BJ tried to open the bar's door, but it was locked.

"Hey!" BJ yelled while honking his horn through the open truck window on the driver's side. "Wake up!"

A few minutes passed before the owner's wife, a plump, easygoing woman whose experience time had etched into facial wrinkles, came through the house's back door. She fixed her mid-shoulder-length flaxen hair as she approached, passed us, and proceeded to the locked door.

"He's just now waking," she stated in a firm voice, her Texas twang permeating each word. "He'll be out in a minute."

We followed her into the bar. The walls were covered with dark, old wood paneling, which created a warm, subdued atmosphere and exuded a musty aroma. It was cold inside, our breath still visible as we spoke.

"What would you like?" she asked.

"Uh ... uh, two Schlitz," BJ said.

She pulled the tabs and placed the beers on the counter. "I better turn on the heat," she stated.

The heaters were two old open-faced gas burners, a copper tube running from the wall to each, with a valve just before the heater. She turned on the gas and ran a lit match over one of the jets. The heat of the blue flames was immediately apparent. My blue jeans soon got hot, although I was five feet away, and I had to move to a side table. BJ stood in front of one heater and turned slowly from side to side, trying to warm up his feet after working all night in the cold.

"Good morning," the owner said as he came through the door.

"Good morning," BJ and I replied.

"BJ, I should've known it was you," he gruffly said, adjusting the brown horn-rimmed glasses that made his eyes appear bigger than they were. "You had to wake me up, didn't you?" he said.

BJ chuckled at his long-time friend. "Quit complaining. We ... we just wanted a beer," he told the owner.

"What else is new?" he sarcastically replied. He looked at me. "Where've you been? I ain't seen you for a while."

"I went out to Virginia, to see my family," I told him.

"H-h-hey!" BJ began. "You know that little store that was robbed in Weimar, last month?"

"Yeah," the owner answered. "They arrested someone for it, didn't they?"

"Well," BJ said, pointing a thumb at me, his fingers curled to his palm, "this is the fellow they arrested."

The owner looked at me suspiciously. "Did ya do it?" he bluntly asked.

"No, I didn't," I stated. "That's why I'm back in Texas. I'm trying to clear it up."

"Why did they arrest you?" he asked.

"Someone identified the truck as mine," I explained, "but I had it with me in Alabama on the date of the crime. I was on my way to Virginia."

"He couldn't have done it," BJ interjected.

"Why do you say 'couldn't'?" the owner replied.

"It's not like him," BJ answered.

"There's a first for everybody," he stated. "Don't say 'couldn't.'"

BJ just shook his head. "Get us another beer, old man," he said, sitting on a stool by the bar. We sat quietly for a moment, enjoying the cold beer's sharp taste.

A truck pulled up to the shack, judging from the sound outside, and someone closed a truck door. The bar door opened and Bryan and Sam entered.

"Get that *damn dog* outta here!" the owner shouted at Bryan.

"He won't be any problem," Bryan loudly told him.

"If he is," the owner replied, "*both* of you leave."

"Okay," Bryan replied. "Fair enough."

He looked down at Sam. "Sam, go lie down." The dog looked up at him wistfully, then walked to a table close to the heater and lay down next to it. "Not there," Bryan stated. "Over by the door." Bryan pointed to the front door. Sam looked at Bryan, and then at the door, and moved to the wall beside the door. He turned to face Bryan once more, and sat on his haunches.

"That's right," Bryan told him. "Lie down." The dog slowly lowered himself to the cold floor.

"I thought I'd find you here," Bryan began. "Mike, do you want to shoot some pool?" He put a quarter into the table.

"Yeah. Why not?" I replied.

BJ began discussing the local deer hunting with the owner. Bryan and I played three or four games, had about as many beers, and then we all returned to the rig.

The bunkhouse was dirty, as usual, the men occupying it indifferent as to its appearance. I put my suitcase under a bunk and lay down. Blankets had been put over the windows to help insulate the place and to block out the light. It was sometimes difficult to sleep during the day, even after working all night.

When BJ and Bryan went to work at eleven that night, I sat down in the doghouse to write a letter to the ACLU, to see if a lawsuit could be brought in this case. BJ walked over to where I was seated.

"Whatcha doin'?" he asked.

"I'm seeing if I can sue the Colorado County police, especially Captain Brooks," I told him.

"Do you think you can?"

"What do you think?"

"Seems like ya should," he answered.

"That's what I think," I told him.

Endings

A dense fog had settled upon the field surrounding the rig. We could not see more than forty feet in any direction. The derrick's lights could not penetrate the mist very well. This quiet dampness muffled the night and hid the dawn. It would not be until ten o'clock the next morning that the sun was able to dissipate the low ceiling.

As the sun tried to penetrate the cover around eight in the morning, I was walking along the edge of the gravel area that had been cleared for the rig. It was on a similar morning, I remembered, that BJ and I had gone "fishing."

He had bought a second-hand little aluminum boat and a small trailer. He had been telling me about his fishing boat and wanted to show me. The rig had been operating near Altair, about forty-five miles west of Houston, off Highway 90. There was this one little creek that ran beneath the Highway 90 overpass. BJ told me that, the day before, he had set out his lines to catch catfish. He brought the trailer and boat by the rig that morning, asking me if I wanted to go collect his catfish.

"Sure, BJ," I told him.

This boat was big enough for two people, but not much more. It was flat-bottomed, with a single seat mounted on a post to the hull, near the stern. It had a tiny little outboard motor, for trolling. BJ was so proud!

When we got to the creek, we carried the boat from the little trailer to the water's edge. The creek was probably thirty yards across at the widest point. We put the boat into the water, with the motor toward the middle of the creek. BJ got in while I steadied the boat, and then I got in, pushing off from the bank.

"Th-th-the lines are on the other side of the overpass," BJ stated, pointing down the creek. "It's a good spot, and I probably got a bunch."

Grinning, I said, "We'll see," over the putt-putting of his little motor. Otherwise, it was a very quiet morning, the fog muffling sounds.

BJ looked at me like I'd hurt his feelings, questioning his "fishing" ability. He knew I was kidding.

We headed down the creek, between the concrete pillars of the highway overpass, and BJ steered the boat to the far bank of the creek. He slowed, reached over to the bank and checked his first line: nothing.

"There'll be some on the next one," he stated, a look of certainty on his face. Now this went on about four more times before he started cursing beneath his breath, and I had begun to make more teasing comments with each empty line.

I think he got two from the whole lot of lines. Finally he had had enough of empty lines and my banter. He turned the boat around, heading back toward the overpass. "The hell with this," he stated. "Let's get us a beer!"

"Now, *that* would be a constructive idea!" I kidded him. His look told me I was being a smartass. I was.

He decided that he would show me what his boat could do. "Watch this!" he told me.

He cranked up that tiny little motor, and the boat picked up speed as we headed toward the gap in the overpass' concrete pillars. We'd gotten to a pretty good speed for such a small motor. BJ guided the boat between the pillars without problem. He was proud! I could see it on his face. Having cleared the pillars, BJ turned the boat motor almost ninety degrees, to redirect the boat toward the bank. I had turned my head, looked ahead of the boat, and then looked back at BJ as I leaned in the direction of the turn.

Suddenly, the post on which BJ's seat rested came loose from the hull, throwing BJ's weight away from the turn. I lost my balance, thrown in the opposite direction by BJ's momentum. The boat flipped!

The water was cold! I came to the surface and began laughing, thinking the failure of BJ's seat pedestal hilarious. Who would have guessed? I looked over in BJ's direction. He was floundering, flailing in the water!

"BJ!" I hollered.

"I can't swim!" he screamed, his head going under.

I swam quickly in his direction. He came to the surface.

"BJ!" I hollered, almost within reach. His arms were flailing without effect. "Don't panic!" I hollered.

Reaching him, I grabbed the shirt sleeve on the downstream arm and pulled it toward me, turning his face away from me as I'd been taught in lifesaving classes, so that he would not attempt to grab me in his fearful state. I stroked once more, throwing my arm by his neck and down, across his chest. BJ continued to struggle. I began side-stroking toward the bank by the truck. BJ kicked and flailed. He was heavy and wet, but we started making progress.

I'd swum perhaps only a dozen and a few more strokes when my foot first touched the creek bed. With the next stroke, I was able to put both feet on the bottom. Turning my back to the shore, I pushed off of the bottom, pulling us both closer to the side. Twice more I did this, and I was standing on the bottom, the water only mid-chest deep. BJ was still kicking and flailing. I started to laugh!

"BJ!" I hollered. No answer: only kicking and flailing. *"BJ!"* I loudly screamed.

"What?!" he hollered, barely able to between gasping breaths.

"Stand up!" I hollered at him.

"What?" he hollered, arms churning water.

"Stand up!" I instructed him. He quit kicking and relaxed his arms. His feet descended to the bottom.

He looked at me. "Shit!" he said, red in the face and breathing hard. I burst out laughing, unable to stop for several minutes.

BJ climbed out of the water while I swam out, righted and retrieved the boat, dragging it behind me by a rope. We put it back on the trailer and secured it. Then BJ opened up the cooler he kept in the back of his truck. He handed me a beer, taking one for himself. We popped the tabs. I looked at him.

"BJ," I said, and he looked at me. "To friends," I stated, lifting the beer in his direction.

The grin on his face was huge. "To friends," he replied.

The air was chilly, and I was starting to shiver. We got back into his truck and, drenched, drove back to the rig. I didn't let him live that story down for a long time. He would just react with this sheepish grin every time I recounted the story.

I glanced around through the fog, as I waited for Bryan this morning. We were going into Sealy so I could call Mr. Paris's office. Sam ran up to me, and I knew Bryan was not far behind. Bryan drove us to a little diner.

"Good morning, Evans and Paris," Sharon stated in her soft Texan way.

"Good morning, Sharon," I replied. "This is Mike Crabtree."

"Yes, Mike," she responded.

"I was supposed to call this morning," I explained.

"Yes, Steve left a message for you," she stated, and then paused. "Let me see . . . oh, yes. You are to take a lie detector test in Huntsville tomorrow."

"What time do we leave the office?" I inquired.

"David will be taking you," she replied. "You will be leaving about 12:30."

"Okay," I told her. "Thanks a lot."

"You're welcome," she replied. "See you tomorrow."

I turned from the pay phone in the little diner. Bryan looked up from his breakfast. "What'd they say?" he managed to say between chews.

"I've got to go to Houston tomorrow," I told him.

"What time?" he asked.

"I should be downtown a few minutes after noon." We were silent for a few moments as we fed our hunger. "I'll catch a bus in the morning," I told him.

"I know where the bus stop is," Bryan replied.

"That's good," I replied, "'cause I don't.'"

We went back to the rig and slept most of the day. I tried to sleep during the night, with some success, as I would need to be alert for the Huntsville trip.

As dawn proceeded and the sun crept above the horizon, gentle, cold breezes silently rearranged the few isolated fog patches remaining. I realized that all of this would soon be over. I could return to Virginia with my head up, having proven my innocence. It was true that I had not yet proven my alibi, as the telephone records were in the billing process and were unavailable. They and the hotel registration would be obtained: it was just a matter of time. Now time, which had become so precious in the anxious acceleration of my uncertain freedom, fell into its normal pace, allowing me to appreciate moments of beauty in the scenery surrounding me.

We got to the bus stop at seven-thirty, only to find that the bus had left at seven-ten. "Oh, hell!" I exclaimed.

"What is it?" BJ asked.

"The bus left twenty minutes ago, and the next one won't get me to Houston in time," I told him.

"That's no problem," BJ replied. "I can run you in."

"That's a sixty mile drive one way," I protested.

"That's not far," he stated. "That won't take but an hour to an hour and a half."

"Okay," I said. "Thanks."

"Yeah," Bryan piped up, from the passenger seat, having been silent to this point. "We want to see you off."

"Let me call home, to tell them what's going on," I said. We went to the diner. I walked over to the pay phone.

"Hello," said the familiar voice.

"Hi, Mom."

"Mike, what's up?" she asked.

"I go in today for a lie detector test," I told her. "If I pass it, I think they'll let me come home."

"That's great, honey," she replied.

"I was hoping to stay a day or two here, to see more of my friends," I stated.

Mom was quiet for a moment, before saying, "We would like to see you as soon as possible ... like tomorrow."

"I understand," I replied. "I'll call this evening."

"Goodbye," my mother said.

"Bye," I said.

Bryan and BJ were seated, awaiting breakfast. "Well," I began, "I'll be going home tomorrow if everything turns out okay."

"Then, we'll *definitely* have to see you to Houston," Bryan stated.

BJ stammered for a moment before finally spurting out, "You coming b-b-back to Texas?"

"I don't know, BJ," I replied. "There's a good chance that I will."

"You know you have a job here anytime," he said.

"Thanks. You've helped me a lot," I told him.

The drive to Houston was quiet, as we had little to say. As we approached the Houston downtown area, its tall buildings seemed out of place on the flat land. When we pulled to the curb in front of the building containing Mr. Paris's office, I hesitated a moment before opening the truck door. I placed my luggage on the sidewalk in front of the building.

"I can't thank y'all enough," I humbly spoke.

"Just do us a favor," Bryan replied with a smile, "and stay the hell out of these things in the future!"

I grinned. "I will if I can," I told them.

BJ reached out his hand. "Y-y-you take care," he said.

"Will do," I replied, shaking his hand.

BJ started his truck and checked his rear-view mirror for an opening in traffic. "Bryan! BJ!" I exclaimed. They turned back toward me. "Watch your hands!"

"Yeah," Bryan firmly replied, nodding, a large, knowing grin on his face.

The most often injured portion of the body while roughnecking was the hand, which was subjected to tremendous beating and stress. It was often said by older oilfield personnel that one was not experienced in the field until one had lost a finger in an accident. There were a multitude of roughnecks with such experience. For this reason, "watch your hands" had become the most heartfelt statement of concern among Bryan, BJ, and me. It was only fitting for me to leave them with that statement of concern for their well-being.

BJ pulled from the curb, and his truck became indistinguishable from the other vehicles moving toward differing destinies. I took my luggage once more into Steve's building.

"Hi, Mike," Sharon said.

"I'm ready to go," I told her.

"It won't be long now," she replied, grinning.

Huntsville was about an hour drive north, on Interstate 45. I was not nervous at all until seeing the red brick walls around Huntsville Prison, where the test was to take place. When David and I entered the building where the tests were to be administered, Captain Brooks was waiting.

The tests were uneventful, as they should have been. All of the questions were "Yes" or "No" answers. After three series of tests, in which different questions were asked, and those pertaining to the crime were changed in sequence, the man administering the tests looked me in the eye.

"This shows that you are telling the truth," he stated.

"*Great!*" I loudly exclaimed. I felt at once like screaming, crying, and laughing!

The officer performing the tests handed the results to Captain Brooks, who was seated nearby. "He passed with flying colors," he told Brooks, whose face suddenly paled.

"I guess," Brooks quietly stated, "that you are free to go." He looked up at me. "The charges against you will not be brought before the Grand Jury," he said.

I was elated, ecstatic! I was free!

The trip back to Houston took too long, although my barrage of questions to David regarding destruction of my police records in Columbus and Virginia Beach seemed to make the time pass more quickly. David told me to come by the office in the morning and settle my account with Evans and Paris. I assured him it would be my pleasure.

R-r-r-ring. "They *have* to be home." R-r-r-ring.

"Hello?" my mother answered.

"Mom!" I replied, barely containing my excitement.

"Yeah, Mike. How'd it go?" she asked.

"I'm *free!*" I loudly proclaimed. "Captain Brooks read the results. The tester told him I was telling the truth. Brooks told me I could go home."

"Oh ... honey," Mom said, between tears. "We knew you were innocent."

"I'll be home tomorrow evening," I told her.

"We'll be waiting," she replied. "Just a minute. Your father wants to talk to you."

Dad got on the line. "Hello, Mike?"

"Yeah, Dad?"

"Congratulations," he stated.

"Thanks," I replied.

"Look ..." he began. "Ask Paris about a suit against Brooks," he instructed me.

"Okay," I said. "I'm to settle the account with him tomorrow."

"What time will you be home?" Mom asked from the other line.

"I don't know. I just got in from Huntsville," I told her. "I'll call you tomorrow, after I talk with Steve and make reservations."

"Okay, hon," Mom replied.

"I'm so happy and relieved!" I told them.

"We are, too," Mom said. "We are for you." We concluded the conversation.

Pam was excited when I told her about my freedom. I told her about my staying at the rig, and about the lie detector test.

"I want to see you," she told me.

"I want to see you, too," I said.

"Can I bring a bottle of wine?" she asked.

"Yes, please!" I replied. "We have something to celebrate." I thought for a second. "One more thing," I told her.

"What's that?" she asked.

"I am going back to Virginia tomorrow," I glumly stated.

"You *are*?" she responded.

"Yes," I quietly answered.

"Are you coming back to Texas later?" she asked.

"I don't know," I replied. "Perhaps."

"I'll see you at eight then, if that's all right," she said.

"That sounds great."

"I'll see you then," she replied. "Bye."

"Bye, Pam."

She was stunning, as usual, when she arrived. She was intelligent, charming, and emotional. We talked for more than an hour. I told her how much I had come to enjoy her company, how she had become very dear to me. We had been seated beside each other at the table, sipping the wine. After some time, we moved to the foot of my bed, where I sat and held her. She had become so dear so quickly. I was going to miss her.

She turned and kissed me. At first it was gentle. We talked and held some more. Her next kiss was not gentle but deeply passionate, and I responded to her spontaneously and without hesitation. When the embrace ended, I stood up, walking halfway across the room.

She walked over in front of me, about a foot away. I kissed her on the side of her face.

"Pam," I said almost breathlessly, my heart pounding. "I'd better let you go home before I lock you in."

She looked into my eyes. "I'm a big girl," she softly stated. "I can take care of myself."

Having said that, she leaned against me, put her hand behind my neck, and pulled my face to hers. I wrapped my arms around her, drawing her closer, kissing her forcefully. Passion seized us both. She began pulling at my shirt and I at her sweater. We were soon on the bed, nothing separating our skin.

Despite the heat of these moments, I could not make love to her. Our breathing was rapid and our hearts racing. Every muscle in my body was screaming for release, but my emotions were not in it. Pam sensed it. She turned on her side and I held her while her breathing slowed, me gently stroking her hair and face. She was so dear, so beautiful. When her breathing slowed to near normal, I moved around in front of her, sitting next to her. I caressed her naked body with the tenderness that I was feeling toward her.

"Pam," I softly said.

"Yes?" she replied.

"You are very dear to me," I told her. "You know and feel that, don't you?"

"Yes," she stated, truthfully.

"I must be honest," I began, but hesitated. "There is someone in Virginia."

"I sort of figured that out," she said, "when you didn't want me."

"She and I are not married or engaged," I told her. "My feelings have never been stronger for her, and she wants me very much. I need to give it every chance to work."

"I understand," Pam quietly said.

"You have quickly become very dear to me, but she and I have a history, and I want to see where it goes," I stated. "I hope you understand."

"I do," she softly replied. Then she said, "I think I should leave."

We got dressed and walked out to her car. She kissed me once, gently, and then wished me good luck. She got into her car and was soon out of sight from the pavement in front of my hotel room. I walked back into the room emotionally frustrated but knowing I had done the right thing for Pam, but mostly for me.

The next morning I opened the door to the office of Evans and Paris. The great oaken doors felt different, although their texture had remained the same. I guess it was my response to their presence that differed. Sharon was busy typing, as usual. "Good morning!" I beamed.

"Hi, Mike!" she replied. "Congratulations!"

"Thank you," I said. "Is Steve in?"

"Yes, Mike," Steve's voice came from his office. "Come on in."

"Steve," I said upon entering, "thank you for everything."

"It's no problem," he replied. "Your parents paid me to do it. I am glad you have proven your innocence. I must say I had some reservations when you first came in."

"That's understandable," I replied.

"Did you want to settle your account?" he asked.

"Yes," I stated. "That and my father wanted me to discuss a lawsuit with you concerning Captain Brooks and the handling of this case."

"Well," Steve said, picking up a pencil with which he began to play. "Mr. Evans, my associate, handles civil law including suits."

Steve spent the next ten minutes describing the pseudo-immunity of the police under the "due cause" stipulation of the rights of detainment. He also said that the superiors and municipality authorizing Brooks's power could not be held responsible for his actions. In all, he made it apparent that a suit against the police was a tedious, drawn-out, and expensive undertaking that often did not warrant the attempt. I took his word as a knowledgeable opinion.

Sharon wrote me a check for the surplus remaining in my parents' account. I cashed it at the next-door bank. I made airline reservations from a nearby telephone, and then called Virginia to advise my parents of the itinerary. My mother was excited on the phone. They would be waiting at the airport.

For some time that afternoon, I again strolled the streets of Houston. It now seemed different.

I stood at last, once more in the Houston terminal, awaiting my flight back to Virginia. It had been a long time coming, this journey, but the delay had reminded me of so much I had let pass in my emotional seclusion over the hurt that Anna had inflicted more than a year ago. I had friends such as Sheriff Smith, BJ and Bryan, Mr. Peter, and a woman who genuinely loved me and wanted me to come back to her. Most importantly, I had the indefatigable support and love of my parents.

There were people I could turn to. That realization was in itself almost worth the ordeal. The flashing line on the departure board announced the boarding of my flight to Norfolk via Atlanta.

The stewardess' perfected smile drew attention away from the exhaustion otherwise apparent upon her face. I found it very difficult to think of anything to say, so the "goodbye" that slipped from between my lips caught me by surprise. "It's *over!*" kept echoing in my head as I walked with tired enthusiasm between and around people in the gate corridor. "Norfolk, at last!" I said to myself. The anticipation of seeing home never seemed greater.

When I saw my parents in the main terminal, it was as if I had just been delivered from death. "I'm *free!*" I announced to them, dropping my bags and giving my mother an enormous hug. Her tears brought my own, despite the smiles on both our faces.

"We're glad it's over," she said as she hugged me. "Welcome home."

Holding her and shaking my father's hand reunited me with them in a closeness I had not known before this all began. My father had never emoted much in my presence, but this incident brought that ability from within him. I cherished it.

The drive home was a continuous series of questions and explanations, my mother curious as to the details of my forced stay in Texas. The talk was not annoying to me, because it allowed me to air my frustration over the entire incident. I had previously cursed the traffic between the Norfolk airport and my parents' home, but tonight was different. Tonight, I was just happy to even see these streets. I was glad to be home but amazed that the entire incident had been real.

I drove by Kempsville High School, looking for Barbara. Her basketball game was over, but I dropped in to see if the principal and vice principal were still inside. Both had heard of my predicament and had expressed concern to my parents. I wanted to let them know it was over. I luckily ran into Mr. Fields, the vice principal, as he exited the gymnasium door. I told him it was all over, and he congratulated me.

The drive to the local high school hangout reminded me of old times, four years earlier, when I enjoyed living in my sphere of innocence. My thoughts wandered to how I had seen, and was watching, the growth of my brothers and sisters, especially Joyce and Barbara. When I entered the hangout, Barbara jumped out of the booth in which she had been sitting, almost knocking over Marty, a cousin of ours, as he tried to get out of her way. She gave me a big, long hug to the disbelief of those who knew her and not me.

We sat back down in her booth. Mike Haskett, who I had not seen in the far corner when I entered, brought over a pitcher of beer. "Welcome back!" he said, shaking my hand. I realized that, yes, it was great to be back. Here I was, at last.

When I called her, Karen was furious at me for not contacting her from Texas, and I took my berating as deserved. I asked to meet her for lunch, to talk with her, and she named a location close to her work.

During the flights, I had debated what I should do now, not about Karen, but about where to live. Having very little money left, I saw little choice but to go back to Texas. I had been told that working offshore, the work schedule was equal time on and off, such as working two weeks and then having two weeks off. That would be an acceptable split, I thought, far better than the moving from town to town, with only two days off at a time. I needed to discuss it with Karen.

When she entered the sandwich shop, she looked very pretty and very professional. I briefly kissed her. She sat down across from me.

"What did you want to talk to me about, Michael?" she asked.

"Karen, this case has taken all of the money that I had saved. I don't see any other choice but for me to go back to Texas to work," I told her.

"I know," she replied.

"I thought that, when I got back there and got set up, I would contact you," I stated.

She paused before speaking. "You keep running away," she said, her tone not loud or excited, just frank. "No, Michael," she began, "you won't contact me." She looked straight into my eyes. "I could have made you very happy. But, you know what? I'm the best thing you'll never have. Do you know the shame about it? You could have, but you gave it away."

With that, she stood. She leaned over, kissing me on the cheek. "Goodbye, Michael." She turned and walked to the door. Without hesitating, she went through it and was gone from my sight.

Epilogue

Several days later, I packed my belongings into the Chrysler Newport Custom. Waving goodbye to my parents and my younger sisters, I pulled away from my parents' home. The drive back to the rig would take twenty-eight hours, which I made stopping only for gas and food. Little did I know the life of adventure that would follow from the decision to return to the oil industry. However, that is a different story.

I learned from all of this that one cannot give up in the "face of adversity." Those times are definitive of what makes each of us the person he or she is. We are the cumulative decisions that we make, and each opportunity is full of unknown possibility. It is never too late to start again, but the first requirement is one's commitment to begin. Lastly, I learned that genuine love requires the honesty and courage to embrace it.

Karen came by for a visit about three years later. By then, I had progressed in the industry and was working a month at a time in western Africa, with the month off being spent at my home outside Austin, Texas. Karen had flown into Austin to visit the family of her fiancé, whose parents had a ranch somewhere nearby. She had come to my house to visit our mutual friend, Terry. He had been one of my roommates in the apartments in Virginia, before I hitchhiked to Texas. When I moved to Austin, he again became my roommate. He kept up with the house when I was at work in Africa. Terry had told me Karen was coming but did not say at what time.

When she arrived, I was in the backyard, mowing my grass. I was hot, sweaty, and unshaven. She walked up to me and kissed me on the cheek. She said she was disappointed that I had not at least showered and shaved to greet her. Perhaps that was best, as we each got what we deserved. She got the happiness that she had so wanted from a man, and I got to convey, if only for a few illusory minutes, that she had not been that important to me.

I did not contact Pam after returning to Texas, as I came to believe that Bryan was right in his assessment. I hoped that she had done well for herself, as she was a beautiful and loving person whose company I immensely enjoyed.

As far as Karen: the last I'd heard, she and her husband had had a child. I hoped that she was able to bear for him at least the second child that she had wanted, and was genuinely happy.